D1433999

Words, Grammar, Text

Benjamins Current Topics

Special issues of established journals tend to circulate within the orbit of the subscribers of those journals. For the Benjamins Current Topics series a number of special issues have been selected containing salient topics of research with the aim to widen the readership and to give this interesting material an additional lease of life in book format.

Volume 18

Words, Grammar, Text. Revisiting the work of John Sinclair
Edited by Rosamund Moon

These materials were previously published in *International Journal of Corpus Linguistics 12:2 (2007)*

Words, Grammar, Text

Revisiting the work of John Sinclair

Edited by

Rosamund Moon

University of Birmingham

John Benjamins Publishing Company

Amsterdam / Philadelphia

™ The paper used in this publication meets the minimum requirements of American National Standard for Information Sciences – Permanence of Paper for Printed Library Materials, ANSI z39.48-1984.

Library of Congress Cataloging-in-Publication Data

Words, grammar, text : revisiting the work of John Sinclair / edited by Rosamund Moon.
    p. cm. (Benjamins Current Topics, ISSN 1874-0081 ; v. 18)
Includes bibliographical references and index.
1. Lexicography. 2. Grammar, Comparative and general. 3. Sinclair, John McHardy,
    1933-2007--Criticism and interpretation. I. Moon, Rosamund.
P327.W67   2009
413.028--dc22   2009017543
ISBN 978 90 272 2248 0 (HB; alk. paper)
ISBN 978 90 272 8925 4 (EB)

© 2009 – John Benjamins B.V.
No part of this book may be reproduced in any form, by print, photoprint, microfilm, or any other means, without written permission from the publisher.

John Benjamins Publishing Co. · P.O. Box 36224 · 1020 ME Amsterdam · The Netherlands
John Benjamins North America · P.O. Box 27519 · Philadelphia PA 19118-0519 · USA

Table of contents

John McHardy Sinclair (14 June 1933 – 13 March 2007)

Introduction

This collection of papers on the work of John Sinclair, Professor of Modern English Language at the University of Birmingham from 1965 until 2000, was first published in 2007 as a special issue of the *International Journal of Corpus Linguistics*. When John died in March 2007, the journal had already passed page-proof stage, and it was impossible then to do more than add an obituary. Inevitably, timing and the nature of the papers meant that it all appeared to be something of a memorial issue, summary commentaries on John's work – something it was never intended to be, and certainly something we never wanted or expected.

In fact, the origins of the papers lie in a series of English Language Research seminars in the Department of English at Birmingham in autumn 2004, which we were later invited to write up for an issue of *IJCL*. Each seminar had looked at a different aspect of John's work, as represented in one or more of his papers, discussing its ideas, and trying to set it in context, both generally in terms of later developments within linguistics, and more narrowly for ongoing work at Birmingham. It was then several years since John had finally retired, nearly ten since he had taught his last class and moved to Italy. John's work, name, and influence were and are still very much in evidence: in the importance put on corpus research, in the references to his work in teaching and on reading lists, and in the annual *Sinclair Lecture* at Birmingham in his honour. There were also still many of us who had worked with John or studied with him. But many others had joined the department or had come here as research students too recently to have known him as a colleague and teacher. Corpus work had become a given rather than a challenge, the sheer radicality of John's work was perhaps understressed or overlooked, and the revolution of the Cobuild project had been dissipated, partly because the rest of the dictionary market had to some extent caught on, and partly because the project itself had disappeared from Birmingham (one colleague commented that he'd never quite understood why there was so much fuss about Cobuild...). The time seemed right to remind ourselves of that challenge, radicality, and revolution.

So our intention in the series of seminars was a return to our department's roots: to take up ideas of John's in order to underline their significance, and to see where they could take us now as researchers and teachers. Some of us well remember the extraordinary seminars of a period in the mid-1980s – perhaps workshops would be a better description – when large groups met each week in a room at

Cobuild to work with John on concordances and argue about why we were seeing the things we did and what those things were; a number of John's papers, such as those on Naturalness, on Collocation, and Sense and Syntax or the Meeting of Lexis and Grammar, are closely associated with that time and record his insights. The headiness of those days could never be matched or recreated without John, but the seminars of autumn 2004 at least generated vibrant discussions of John's ideas, and recognition of their creativity and importance. While the full range of John's work could not be covered in a single semester, those seminars, and the written versions included here, looked at some key areas, in particular John's writings on words, grammar, and text, and running through all those, his concerns with meaning and with the corpus.

When John heard about the 2004 seminar series, he was tolerant and humorous. He accepted the intrusion, and graciously commented on our *IJCL* papers, helping us with many points and questions. In a preface to that issue, he said of us as authors '...the sum of their gentle criticisms felt like an end-of-term report "Could try harder"'; and later 'I see this in part as their gentle exorcism, a final evaluation of my work'. I think for us it was quite the opposite: we were keen to check the extent to which our interpretations of John's work accorded with his vision. Far from exorcising or summing up a life's work, we were re-invoking it and trying to show how much there was still to learn, how important it was for us to engage with John's ideas. John also said in that preface

> Now I have very little time for any work, including my own backlist, which is not rooted in the actual patterns of occurrence of words in text.

and later:

> A recurrent theme in the papers is the attitude I have to corpus evidence; the corpus has things to tell me, and I try to work out where it is heading. I have been surprised at the confidence of so many scholars, who seem to think that they have something to tell the corpus.

Of all John's comments, this is perhaps the most important and enduring: as he put it elsewhere, 'we should trust the text. We should be open to what it may tell us.'

In this collection, the original *IJCL* papers are republished unchanged, apart from a few corrections and the addition of afterwords. The order of papers is also unchanged, with the topic sequence moving from word through grammar to text. As far as possible, the versions of John's papers discussed here are those appearing in one of the collections *Corpus, Concordance, Collocation* (1991, Oxford University Press) and *Trust the Text* (2004, Routledge), for ease and consistency of reference.

Rosamund Moon
Birmingham, March 2009

Sinclair, lexicography, and the Cobuild Project

The application of theory

Rosamund Moon
University of Birmingham

This paper discusses John Sinclair's work in the field of lexicography by focussing on the first edition of the *Collins Cobuild English Language Dictionary* (1987), which was written within the Department of English at the University of Birmingham, and of which Sinclair was Editor in Chief. It provides theoretical and lexicographical background to the Cobuild Project, and reviews aspects of the first dictionary which were especially innovative, including its corpus basis, treatment of phraseology, and approach to the representation of meaning. It concludes by reflecting on the overall impact of Cobuild and Sinclair's ideas.

Keywords: lexicography, Cobuild Project, corpus evidence, meaning, definitions, lexicogrammar

1. Preamble

Without a doubt, John Sinclair's most important contribution to lexicography is the *Collins Cobuild English Language Dictionary* (CCELD), first published in 1987. As a reference book, it was bought and used by several million people around the world — language learners, teachers, translators, researchers — and so too were its succeeding editions. As a text, it had a massive impact on the practice of commercial dictionary-making, on metalexicography and lexicographical theory, and beyond that on language description in general.

Much of the following discussion concerns the radical nature of CCELD and ways in which Sinclair's ideas were channelled through the Cobuild project in lexical computing.[1] It took less than seven years — just sixty-four months, in fact, between the main start-up of the Cobuild project in 1981 and the completion of the CCELD dictionary text in 1986 — for the lexicographical world to be transformed. In the ten years following CCELD's publication, over fifty titles were added to the Cobuild range, with a number winning awards. Yet it is salutary to remember that in July 1997, three-quarters of the then Cobuild team were made redundant, and the project as such abandoned. Editorial control of the Cobuild range moved from Birmingham to HarperCollins' dictionaries department in Glasgow, and Cobuild's dominant ethos, where linguistic research according to Sinclairian principles was realized in dictionary output, was finally subordinated to the commercial realities of dictionary publishing in a competitive global market. This is the fascinating irony of the Cobuild project, that its creativity did not lead to the kind of financial success which could have secured its survival in its original research-led form.

This paper is, necessarily, a personal evaluation of Sinclair's contribution to lexicography and of CCELD and the Cobuild project: I worked on the project from its main start-up, and I was one of the editors of CCELD, along with Patrick Hanks (as managing editor), Gwyneth Fox, and the late Penny Stock. Nearly thirty years have elapsed since Cobuild began, and it is now difficult to present an account which is not revisionist and influenced by later developments at Cobuild and elsewhere. Yet it is also too easy, nearly thirty years on, for the significance, radicality, and sheer excitement of the original Cobuild project to be overlooked, and that would be unjust.

My aim, then, in this paper is to show what Sinclair and Cobuild did, and why CCELD developed in the way it did. Cobuild was, of course, a team project: Sinclair as director was instrumental in formulating principles which became part of Cobuild lexicographical orthodoxy, but developmental work and implementation was done by the Cobuild team, drawing on their skills, including in most cases extensive experience in lexicography, linguistics, languages, pedagogy, or computing. It is only appropriate to acknowledge here the contributions of the team itself, of Hanks, Fox, and Stock, Jeremy Clear, and others in the first years of the project, with further input from Sinclair's sister Sue Atkins and from Sinclair's colleagues at the University of Birmingham, including Michael Hoey and David Brazil.

2.   Metalexicography: theory and principle

To contextualize the theoretical background to the Cobuild project, I want first to look at Sinclair's paper 'Lexicography as an academic subject' (1984a) which he had delivered as a keynote address at the first EURALEX congress in September 1983. Historically, the Cobuild project had started, but was only one-third of the way through its ground-breaking period, and under threat of closure. More widely, there was a divide in Britain between lexicographical practioners, who were mostly atheoretical linguistically, and theorists, who were mostly uninterested in lexicographical methodology and practice.

Sinclair (1984a) can be seen as a reaction to the abstractness of lexicographical theory at a time when metalexicographers were beginning to organize themselves into an international association on the model of other learned or professional associations: a warning, perhaps, that the status quo needed to be re-examined by both theorists and practitioners. In exploring its central question — whether lexicography is suitable as an academic subject — the paper argued that a much broader view needed to be taken of what lexicography involves. It situated lexicography as an applied subject at the intersection of information technology (linked to computational linguistics), general linguistics (not limited to semantics), and what Sinclair termed 'experience', or expertise in and awareness of the practical issues of dictionary compilation. Before fleshing out a syllabus for a masters-level course in lexicography which drew on these areas, he commented "There is, for example, no subject heading 'Lexicography theory' in my syllabus because I have nothing to put there" (Sinclair 1984a:6) and further

> ... it seems necessary to keep on stressing:
> (a) that the study of lexicography includes the practice of it;
> (b) that there is no prospect of a theory of lexicography. (ibid:7)

The insistence on the absence of lexicographical theory, however, has to be taken alongside Sinclair's recognition of the principles of lexicographical practice, whether actual or desired. This in turn contextualizes the ideology which informed Cobuild methodology: it was principled and not atheoretical.

The main interest in this paper lies now not in the proposed academic syllabus but in objections which Sinclair raised to the existing state of affairs in lexicography. Because lexicography is not properly an academic study, there is no real structure for external evaluation, so that lexicography becomes "introspective and conservative" and "in danger of narrowing down its range of expertise, and reducing its flexibility" (1984a:5). Because practical lexicography is project-specific and training occurs within the context of existing projects, there is no real opportunity for "speculation and experiment" (1984a:5), and no impetus for developing general principles. Lexicography as a practical skill needs to be put "on the intellectual map", and only then can its traditions and principles be properly evaluated in the light of "contributory and contingent" disciplines (that is, information technology and general linguistics) (1984a:4) — thus, it is implied, enabling innovations in dictionary practice. Sinclair discusses particular features of dictionaries which could be investigated, querying whether they are "inherent" or "accidental": these include the substitutability of definitions; the notion of 'sense'; the treatment of syntax; typography; and the use of concocted, non-authentic illustrative examples. In the course of the Cobuild project, all these features were to be re-evaluated: see further in Section 5.

While arguing for lexicography to become further principled and for those principles to be drawn from external disciplines, Sinclair also turned the argument on its head. He pointed out that lexicographers, more than any other group, work with usage, though still lacking "sufficient formalism to influence linguistics" (1984a:11), and he looked forward to a time when observations drawn from a principled applied discipline of lexicography feed back into theory:

> The uneasy, ill-fitting abstractions of the linguists who worked with just their intuitions and a few scraps of evidence will have an opportunity to be reformulated, retaining their positive insights. And perhaps some startling new concepts will emerge from the interaction between Computational Linguistics and Lexicography.
> (Sinclair 1984a:11–12)

Twenty-one years later, in a second keynote address to a EURALEX congress, Sinclair talked of a theory of meaning developed from just such an interaction: see Sinclair (2004b), and the brief discussion in Section 7 below.

3.   The context of the Cobuild project

From the outset, the intention behind the Cobuild project was to build a corpus of current English and to use this to produce a monolingual learner's dictionary to compete with the Oxford and Longman titles, as part of a whole range of books for learners of English. Cobuild in fact occurred at a critical juncture in relation to developments in both linguistic methodology and lexicography. While corpus linguistics had effectively begun in the 1960s with the creation of the 1-million word Brown and LOB corpora, computing power and expertise in the humanities were still scarce in the late 1970s: relatively few linguists had access to corpus evidence and were in a position to explore its possibilities. The decision to use a corpus as a basis for a dictionary was therefore innovative technologically as well as lexicographically, and inevitably involved experimentation. Collins publishers had themselves been innovative in the 1970s, producing pace-setting, very different bilingual dictionaries (*Collins Spanish Dictionary* (1971); *Collins-Robert French-English Dictionary* (1978)), and a new kind of monolingual dictionary for native speakers (*Collins English Dictionary* (1979)): the second and third of these had been spearheaded by respectively Sue Atkins and Patrick Hanks, whose expertise at Cobuild was crucial. There had also been changes within the publishing world with respect to dictionaries for learners of English. The first such dictionary, the *Idiomatic and Syntactic English Dictionary* (published in Tokyo in 1942) was edited by Hornby, Gatenby, and Wakefield, and based on extensive experience of teaching in Japan and a recognition of the importance of collocation and syntactic patterning in a pedagogical context. It was retitled and republished in 1948 by Oxford University Press, and along with its second edition in 1963, dominated a growing EFL market. The third edition (the *Oxford Advanced Learner's Dictionary of Current English*) appeared in 1974, and nothing compared with it for prestige or coverage, though there were other learners' dictionaries in the market, including one published by Collins (*Collins English Learner's Dictionary* (1974)). However, in 1978, the first real rival for Oxford appeared, the innovative *Longman Dictionary of Contemporary English*, which brought a learner's perspective as well as a teacher's perspective to lexicography and, introduced a controlled defining vocabulary, so that all words in the dictionary were defined through a limited lexicon of approximately 2000 words.[2]

What the Cobuild project did was to exploit these various strands: to produce a completely new dictionary for learners, based on corpus evidence, while discarding or at least questioning lexicographical conventions, for a market which had already been shaken up.

3.1 The impact of Collins Cobuild English Language Dictionary

The radical nature of CCELD and its impact on lexicography can be shown by looking at the treatments of the noun *impact* itself in learners' dictionaries which predated the publication of CCELD in 1987. In these and other dictionary entries quoted below, phonetics are omitted and typography is only an approximate representation of that in the original text.

> **impact** *n* ~ (on), 1 [C] collision. 2 [U] force exerted by one object when striking against another: *The car body collapses on* ~, when it collides with sth. 3 strong impression or effect: *the* ~ *of new ideas on discontented students.*
> (*Oxford Advanced Learner's Dictionary*, ed 3, 1974)

> **impact** *nc* 1. force of two things hitting each other; collision. *When the car hit the wall, the impact broke the windscreen.* 2. influence; impression. *This book had | made a great impact on its readers.* (*Collins English Learner's Dictionary*, 1974)

> **impact** *n* 1 the force of one object hitting another 2 the force of an idea, invention, system, etc. 3 **on impact** at the moment of hitting.
> (*Longman Dictionary of Contemporary English*, ed. 1, 1978)

The second edition of the Longman dictionary, published in the same year as CCELD, had extended and enhanced its entry, though it was still similar in structure:

> **impact** *n* 1 the force of one object hitting another 2 [(on)] an esp. strong or powerful influence or effect caused or produced by an idea, invention, event, etc.: *The*

> *computer has had|made a great impact on modern life.* | *The full impact of these*
> *changes has not yet been felt.* **3 on impact** at the moment of hitting: *The cup hit the*
> *wall and broke on impact.*
>
> (*Longman Dictionary of Contemporary English*, ed. 2, 1987)

The corresponding entry in CCELD is as follows:

> **impact 1** The **impact** that something has on a situation, process, person, etc is
> the effect that it has on it. EG *The new seeds had an immediate impact on food*
> *production...the impact of computing on routine office work... British authors make*
> *relatively little impact abroad.*
>
> **2 Impact** is **2.1** the action of one object hitting another, usually with a lot of force.
> EG *Many modern bullets produce an explosive effect upon impact... The estimated*
> *point of impact of each missile was worked out by computer.* **2.2** the force with
> which one object hits another. EG *Hill 402 seemed to crumble with the impact of*
> *enemy artillery fire.*

It is a longer entry: particularly important is the sequence of senses, with the more
abstract sense preceding more concrete ones, thus reflecting frequency of usage
and not a historical or logical semantic development. Compare the entry in the
post-corpus edition of the Longman dictionary, where the order of senses has
been reversed:

> **impact** *n* [C] **1** the effect or influence that an event, situation etc has on someone
> or something: *the environmental impact of increased road traffic* | **have an impact**
> **(on)** *Warnings about the dangers of smoking seem to have little impact on this age*
> *group.* **2** the force of one object hitting another: *The impact pushed the engine*
> *backwards and crushed my legs.* **3 on impact** at the moment when one thing hits
> another: *a missile which explodes on impact*
>
> (*Longman Dictionary of Contemporary English*, ed. 3, 1995)

Entries in later editions of Oxford, Longman, and other learners' dictionaries
have similar sequencing of senses and level of detail. Overall, there has been a
major shift in philosophy and approach: in particular, greater explicitness (including fewer abbreviations), the prioritization of frequency, and an indication of the
dominant lexicogrammatical patterns associated with the object word — just as in
Cobuild orthodoxy.

4.   Corpus and dictionary

Work towards CCELD was underpinned by the principle that it should be a record of how language was actually used, not thought to be used, with this record

constructed from corpus evidence. Other dictionaries — most notably Johnson's *Dictionary of the English Language* (1755) and the *Oxford English Dictionary* (1884–1928) — had been based on thorough examinations of evidence, though this evidence consisted of collections of citations: a methodology prone to unrepresentativeness. Most dictionaries, however, were based on a mixture of citations, introspection, and what other dictionaries said. Not only would a corpus provide a more objective source of evidence, it would enable, even enforce, a new look at the language, in particular the lexicon of approximately 30,000–40,000 simplex lemmas which comprises the target headword list of learners' dictionaries. Sinclair commented:

> The general conclusion is that much more precision can be gained in lexicography by studying instances, even in the earliest stages, where we are doing little more than gathering instances together. There is at present hardly any relevant theory to guide us, and further advances can be expected with the formulation of theoretical positions — on collocational structure, on the constitution of a phrase, on the interaction between structure and sense. This should be paralleled by technical developments in our ability to handle and analyse the instances. The room for development in lexicography is enormous.   (Sinclair 1985:91)

(The formulation of the theoretical positions in relation to CCELD's treatment of sense, syntax, and phraseology is discussed in Section 5.)

Corpora are now commonplace as lexicographical resources; however, they have created their own problems. One is that it is hugely time-consuming to analyse corpus data, and therefore hugely expensive for commercial dictionary budgets. Another is that corpora have grown too large to analyse with the kind of methodology developed during the initial stages of the Cobuild project, when lexicographers worked with paper printouts of corpus lines and when the corpus was just 7.5 million words in all, so that in many cases there were only a few instances of each lemma. For example, there were 35 tokens of the noun/verb lemma *skate*; in contrast, the 450-million word Bank of English has almost 5000 tokens, which makes it impossible to analyse except through sampling and the use of profiling software. *Skate* has several uses, and it is unlikely that a corpus lexicographer would look at fewer than 50–100 instances, but even a sample as small as this automatically increases the time taken for analysis, while rarer uses have to be searched for separately. A third problem, perhaps, is that there is still no perfect understanding of how far corpora and their component texts map onto the language as a whole and onto the language to which users are exposed in everyday life — neither of which are homogeneous or static entities. A fourth problem arises from the very task of corpus analysis: the copious evidence of recurrent phraseological patterning and specific collocates encourages a proliferation of semi-lexicalized phrases and context- or collocate-specific senses in dictionaries based on that evidence. Certainly, in the case of CCELD, generalities were sometimes lost, and entries became too diffuse and complicated for the target users and their reference needs, even though they reflected the language data observed, and accorded with an intuitively satisfactory model of language. This was perhaps the hardest and saddest lesson to be learnt: that a purist approach to corpus data did not necessarily lead to better dictionaries, and other issues, such as the constraints of presenting information to users within a dictionary format, had to be accepted.

Sinclair was not unaware of all these issues:

> ...The corpus of the 1980s, although boasting a central size of 20 million words, will be seen in another decade as a relatively modest repository of evidence... Most limiting of all, our concepts, our ideas of what to expect and and how to understand what we are observing, are not keeping pace with the evidence available. There is as yet little or no discussion at an international level and, beyond the Cobuild project, no thorough exploitation of corpus linguistics. (Sinclair 1991:137)

But some fifteen years later, the issues had scarcely been resolved, certainly not in relation to lexicography. Sinclair's concept of using a corpus has, however, been vindicated.

5.   Lexicographical innovations in CCELD

In drawing attention to traditional dictionary features which seemed due for reevaluation (definitions, the notion and analysis of sense, syntax, typography, exemplification), Sinclair (1984a) signalled aspects of Cobuild lexicography where innovations were under development. The following looks at these features in the light of how they were realized in CCELD by the Cobuild team. See also the detailed critiques by Cowie (1999:118ff), and, in relation to the four learners' dictionaries of 1995 (new editions of CCELD, Longman, and Oxford, and a new dictionary from Cambridge), the extended reviews by Bogaards (1996) and Herbst (1996), along with the collection of papers edited by Herbst and Popp (1999).

5.1   Sense and syntax, form and phraseology

It became central to the Cobuild approach to the analysis of lexis that sense and syntax had to be closely linked. In his 1984 EURALEX paper, Sinclair had commented:

> ...the activity of lexicography is dominated by sense in the sense of "substance or gist: meaning". Sense divisions, sense groupings, etc. are the main focus of attention. Other matters tend to be secondary, and can become rudimentary or even self-contradictory. In most lexicography, matters of syntax are rudimentary and even in pedagogical lexicography they are secondary... We must ask if this is a balanced view.
>
> (Sinclair 1984a:4)

This could simply suggest a need for a realignment of the relative importance of sense and syntax, and for a fuller integration of grammatical information into the descriptions of individual senses of individual words. Certainly, Sinclair's interest in grammar and a need for CCELD to deal with grammar in at least as much detail as the Oxford and Longman learners' dictionaries had meant that syntax had always been a priority.

However, the notion of syntax became associated with form in general: the form of the actual item or use under investigation, the syntactic structures in which it occurred, and its collocates. This led to an inversion of the importance of form and sense, with sense being secondary, cf. Sinclair's assertion "Every distinct sense of a word is associated with a distinction in form" (cited in Sinclair 1987:89).

Thus ambiguity of a word in the terms of traditional semantics is impossible: either something in the context disambiguates (with that something including intonation, speaker's intention, and shared knowledge where appropriate), or else the word is not ambiguous and therefore requires a more general definition than had been given. It is always possible to find or invent examples which disprove this, yet corpus lexicography generally supports it. Most corpus tokens, even in a restricted concordance format, are interpretable: of those which are not, most simply need extended contexts and only a very few are aberrant uses outside the general lexicon of English and thus certainly beyond the scope of CCELD.

The emphasis on form and downplay of independent meaning is a logical result of using corpus evidence in lexicography. Lexicogrammatical patterns are foregrounded and used to identify the different meanings of polysemous words. Moreover, it becomes difficult to detach meanings or uses of very common words such as *take, know, fact,* or *time* from the patterns in which they occur. Evidence shows that their most frequent uses are often delexicalized: thus semantically independent meanings of *take* such as 'remove, move, steal, escort' are less common than its use in structures such as *take a step, take part, take a long time*. As a result, CCELD needed to put a special emphasis on phraseological patterning and to build information about form into the descriptions of meaning. This was done in three ways: through the formulaic syntactic information in the extra column (see 5.4), through examples which reflected patterning (see 5.3), and through a particular approach to definition (see 5.2).

The priority which Cobuild put on phraseology — the interdependence of form and meaning, a sensitivity to collocation, lexicogrammar, and context — is one of its great strengths. Hornby et al had made a special feature of phraseological patterning in their first learner's dictionary (*Idiomatic and Syntactic English Dictionary*) some forty years earlier, though the patterning was identified from experience of language and language teaching. Cobuild had a corpus and the evidence to see what the patterns were. CCELD represents one output: other, theoretical, outputs include Sinclair's model of collocation and language structure, the co-existing open choice and idiom principles (Sinclair 1991:109–112; see also Barnbrook, this volume), and Hunston and Francis's model of pattern grammar (2000), which grew out of work undertaken on the grammatical coding for CCELD's second edition. The weakness, however, was in the application. There were, as already mentioned, too many dubious minor senses or recurrent patterns presented as fixed phrases. Furthermore, CCELD, in spite of its linguistic knowledge and best efforts, did not always succeed in indicating collocation sufficiently clearly for the end-user: for example, which words in definitions or examples realized specific collocates and which were simply typical, hyponymic, or symbolic. In

> If you **distort** a statement or an argument, you change it so that its meaning becomes different.
>
> Colours that are **strong** are very bright and intense.

the status of *statement, argument, colours* is indeterminate, and the accompanying examples do little to indicate range and restriction. Other dictionaries in the post-corpus era have made the overt indication of phraseology a special feature, though the impetus there has been the needs of the learner-user, not an ideology.

5.2 Definitions and explanations

Sinclair's EURALEX comments on traditional definitions were as follows:

> Take the principle of substitutability, for example. Is it possible to show that the following of this principle leads to definitions which have positive attributes of clarity, conciseness and precision, other things being equal; and conversely that the breaking of it leads to faulty definition? Are there intermediate positions which would recommend following it in certain circumstances and following an alternative strategy in other, clearly identified, circumstances?
> (Sinclair 1984a:3–4)

At this point in the project, definitions were still being formulated in a traditional way. Phrases were glossed in context, rather in the way that short examples are given translations in bilingual dictionaries; definitions of other items reflected word class and were broadly substitutable, although there had been some debate about how best to reflect selectional restrictions, valency, and context. (Compare the standard dictionary techniques, as for *fair* '(with reference to the weather) without rain' and for *serve* 'give something that is required (esp. to a customer in a shop)': these definitions are from *Collins English Learner's Dictionary* (1974).) The theory which underlies substitutability of definitions is that it should be possible to replace the item or sense being defined, in its context, by the definition without any loss or change of meaning. This implies that the item or sense has an isolatable meaning, a meaning in isolation, yet the lexicographical analysis of corpus data at Cobuild was making it clear that meanings were tied up with context and identifiable through patterning. It became increasingly obvious that new techniques were needed here too in order to represent better the lexical truths being observed.

The solution adopted was that of defining words in context, in full sentences which indicate context and lexicogrammatical patterning. This approach to definition — or explanation, the preferred term — came to characterize CCELD and other dictionaries produced by the Cobuild project. For example[3]:

> When it is **fair**, the weather is pleasant, dry, and fine.

> If someone **serves** customers in a shop, bar, etc, they help them and provide them with what they want to have or buy.

> A **desert island** is a small tropical island where nobody lives.

> If you feel **stress** or if you are under **stress**, you feel tension and anxiety because of difficulties in your life.

> **Torrential** rain pours down very rapidly and in great quantities.

> If you say that a period of time **goes** quickly, slowly, etc, you mean that it seems to pass in that manner.

> If you say something **in jest**, you do not mean it seriously, but want to be amusing.

> You can also use **at least** when you want to modify or correct something that you have just said.

> If you talk about something in economic **terms,** in political **terms,** etc, you are specifying which aspect of a situation you are concerned with.

> If you do something **with** a particular object, tool, or other thing, you do it using that object, tool, or thing.

> You can call someone **pet** as a sign of affection or friendliness; an informal use.

Over the course of editing CCELD, a range of such techniques developed. By abandoning substitutability, it was possible not only to indicate context, pattern, and usage, but to avoid any implication that meaning exists in isolation of context. See Hanks (1987), Sinclair (1991:123–137), and Barnbrook (2002) for further discussion of Cobuild definitions.

The technique of full-sentence definitions was not of course invented by Cobuild, and historically it can be associated with early monolingual dictionaries and children's dictionaries, as well as folk definitions or informal definition in spoken interaction. For example, Johnson used it to explain restricted collocations and phrases in *A Dictionary of the English Language* (1755):

> To *keep pace*, is not to be left behind.

> *I believe*, is sometimes used as a way of slightly noting some want of certainty or exactness.

The following are taken from a children's dictionary of 1967, *Picture Dictionary*, published by Burke:

> A **half** is one of two equal parts of something.

> If we are **last**, we are behind everyone else.

> We **live** when we breathe and are full of life.

At their best, Cobuild definitions provide a clear way of showing the linguistic environment of words from both structural and discoursal points of view; at their worst, as critics commented, they are rambling and unclear. Because the technique was used for all words, a particular consequence was that Cobuild dictionaries were either much longer compared with competing titles or had fewer headwords. In the case of CCELD, it was not only physically larger than its rivals but had no room for pictorial illustrations: both disadvantages from the marketing point of view. While other publishers of learners' dictionaries did not follow Cobuild's model in the same way, the technique has been used in many cases to show co-textual restrictions, and the following, for example, are taken from the *Macmillan English Dictionary* (2002):

> torrential rain falls hard and fast.

> if time goes in a particular way, it passes in that way.

> if you say something in jest, you do not mean it seriously.

As already mentioned, a major innovation of the first *Longman Dictionary of Contemporary English* (1978) had been the introduction of a restricted vocabulary for definitions. Early work on the Cobuild project had included the development of a set of controls for definition language: this was superseded by the principle of explaining words in context, but in practice, definitions in CCELD and later Cobuild dictionaries used a core vocabulary of around 2500–3000 items. This is consistent with that used in other learners' dictionaries, which have followed Longman's example and made a restricted defining vocabulary a key feature in marketing. Something of the effect of this on Cobuild dictionaries can be seen by comparing the back cover blurb on definitions in CCELD

> Each separate sense explained in a sentence to show essential grammar

and its counterpart in CCELD's second edition

> Carefully selected defining vocabulary

though the changes in the dictionary itself were largely in terms of refining the original definition style, rather than the imposition of a limited vocabulary, and the market failed to be convinced.

5.3 Dictionary examples

Learners' dictionaries had generally relied on examples to show typical contexts of use, including structures and collocations, and for the most part these were constructed by lexicographers themselves. Sinclair (1984a:4) argues that such examples "are of no value at all. It can be claimed that they illustrate the word in use, but one thing we do know is that usage cannot be thought up — it can only occur".

The very unnaturalness of made-up examples was the subject of Sinclair's paper 'Naturalness in language' (1984b), which explored the relationship between (grammatical) well-formedness and naturalness or idiomaticity, and established criteria for why syntactically correct examples (as in a textbook or dictionary) may be atypical of natural language. Relevant factors are that concocted examples may be too dense informationally and lack the cohesive links found in real language; they may not realize the kinds of pattern which occur in corpora; and they may be unlikely for pragmatic reasons, such as the improbability of a discoursal context where such utterances might occur. The following examples, cases in point, are drawn from *Collins English Learner's Dictionary* (1974):

> (for *challenge*) The soldier on guard challenged the strangers who tried to come in.

> (for *designate*) The Prime Minister has designated three new members of his government.

> (for *sputter*) The hot iron sputtered when we put water on it.

It was always the intention that examples in CCELD would be drawn from the corpus, either unedited or at most only lightly edited. Corpus examples would not

only replicate the kinds of textual context which learners would be likely to encounter, but would better reflect pattern. The extended explanations or definitions,
incorporating lexicogrammatical patterning in a neutral context, would themselves fulfil the role that very simple made-up examples had in other pedagogical
dictionaries.

> (for *challenge*) If you **challenge** someone… you order them to stop and tell you
> who they are or why they are there. EG *The party was challenged by the sentry:
> 'Halt! Who comes there?'*

> (for *designate*) If you **designate** someone… you formally choose them to do a
> particular job. EG *The President designated Hussein as his successor… I had been
> designated to read the lesson.*

> (for *sputter*) If something, for example an engine, **sputters**, it makes soft hissing
> and popping sounds. EG *Then the engine began coughing and popping and sputter-
> ing… The fire sputtered quietly.*

See Fox (1987) for a discussion of the rationale and implementation.

The logic of using corpus examples was clear, yet the results were often disap-
pointing, and contributed to the general lengthiness of the dictionary in comparison with its competitors. The purist approach was not adopted by other learners'
dictionaries, which typically use corpus patterns as a model for their own simpli-
fied examples. In the market, only very high-level learners and language profes-
sionals (translators, teachers, etc.) really appreciated the examples: younger, lower-
level users found them too difficult and often bewildering. It was unfortunate that
CCELD examples which had seemed entirely clear to lexicographers, who had the
benefit of extended contexts, were sometimes unclear, unhelpful, distracting, or
bizarre when isolated within a dictionary entry:

> (for *carpet*) He asked what the marks were on the stair carpet.

> (for *matter/matters*) The murder of Jean-Marie will not help matters.

> (for adjectival *pet*) We were listening to yet another gardener with his pet theories.

> (for *tumble*) At any moment you may tumble to irreversible ruin.

5.4 Typography

Typography is only mentioned by Sinclair in an aside in his EURALEX address:
"The more minute typographical distinctions, for example, may be savoured
by fellow lexicographers, but ignored or misinterpreted by users" (1984a:4).
However, the importance of re-evaluating typographical conventions had been

acknowledged from the beginning. This included the use of codes and abbreviations, brackets and other punctuation devices, and different fonts. Some conventions were retained, such as bold font for headwords: the widespread use of italics
for illustrative examples was also retained, although in CCELD examples were
also signalled by EG. Many other dictionary conventions had originally developed
as space-saving devices (codes for grammar, abbreviations such as *fml* to indicate
register, swung dashes to avoid repetitions of a headword) but the resulting entries were often messy, as in these entries for the verb *envy* (the headword **envy**[1]
dealt with the noun):

> **envy**[2] *vt* (*pt, pp* -vied) [VP6A, 12C] feel ENVY of: *I ~ you. I ~ your good fortune. I
> don't ~ him his bad-tempered wife*, am glad I am not married to her. (*Oxford Ad-
> vanced Learner's Dictionary*, ed. 3, 1974)

> **envy**[2] *v* [W v4, 5; D1; T1] to feel ENVY (1) for or of: *I don't envy you your journey
> in this bad weather* -~**ingly** *adv* (*Longman Dictionary of Contemporary English*,
> ed. 1, 1978)

In contrast, CCELD had a single entry for noun and verb uses, with the latter as
follows:

> 2 If you **envy** someone, you wish that you had the same things or qualities that
> they have. EG *You know, I envy a person like Jaykar very much… It would be unfair
> to envy him his good fortune.*

Formal grammatical information was given in a narrow column — the extra column — to the right of each column of text, thus removing abbreviated, non-dis-
cursive information from the main discursive text in order to give a cleaner appearance to the page. This verbal use of *envy* was labelled as V+O, or V+O+O: the
intention being that abbreviations should be as explicit as possible.

Since the publication of CCELD, other learners' dictionaries have moved towards greater typographical simplicity and an avoidance of abbreviations within
the bodies of entries. There is increasing use of secondary colour or full four-co-
lour printing and perhaps a better appreciation of the need for white space in
dictionary text (to avoid dense blocks of text which are difficult to navigate). There
has also been a move away from highly codified grammatical information: abbreviations are minimalistic and relatively self-evident (for example, V, N, adj, n
plural), and structures are often explicitly shown as patterns. The benefits for users
are obvious, although in order to compensate for the greater lengthiness of entries,
dictionaries have either become larger or have lost some kinds of information,
such as peripheral words and senses, or grammatical detail.

6.   The fuller picture: the treatment of common words

All the strands of lexicographical innovation and experimentation at Cobuild came together in the treatment of common words. The corpus evidence for relatively simple items such as *skate* largely corroborated rather than challenged the kinds of received ideas about its meaning and usage to be found in pre-corpus dictionaries. The real excitement at Cobuild came with high frequency items, where the corpus provided massive evidence of what these central items were and how they were used syntactically, collocationally, and pragmatically. The pedagogical importance is obvious, since the acquisition of competence in another language depends on competence with its central vocabulary. As Sinclair commented in the introduction to CCELD:

> The evidence that is accumulating suggests that learners would do well to learn the common words of the language very thoroughly because they carry the main patterns of the language. The patterns have to be rather precisely described in order to avoid confusion, but then are capable of being rather precisely deployed...
> (1987:159)

So one area which the Cobuild project had needed to address was to how to deal with common words and how to represent their patterns as observed. Entries had to make it clear that the meanings of common words — usually with multiple senses, and in 500 or so cases, with a dozen or more senses or phrases — were differentiated through phraseology and the co-text. Lexicographers therefore had to exploit fully the potential of full-sentence definitions, to illustrate usages with copious examples, and to make sure that dictionary design and typography made the structures and content of entries as clear as possible. The most obvious result in CCELD was the length of entries for these words. For example, CCELD's entry for *fact* (one of the top 300–400 words in general English) fills half a page, over 80 lines of text, and has 15 defined senses. Many are tied to phraseological patterns, and they include explanation of discoursal uses as preface, as in *The fact is, I don't really want to go*, and as a cohesive general noun (Halliday & Hasan 1976:274ff), as in *He is really not amused but wishes to hide the fact*[4]. For comparison, entries in the pre-corpus 1974 Oxford or 1978 Longman dictionaries were less than a quarter of the length, the only phraseologies discussed were expressions such as *as a matter of fact* and *the facts of life*, and the cohesive uses were not described. Overall, the impression was that the word *fact* was no more significant than words such as *romantic, verse,* or indeed *skate,* which took up roughly the same amount of space. In contrast, post-corpus learners' dictionaries have long, detailed entries for *fact,* showing discoursal uses and semi-lexicalized phraseologies, and making clear that it is a priority item.

Sinclair and the Cobuild project were not unique in drawing attention to common words and their importance for the learner: compare the work done by West and Hindmarsh in drawing up word lists for ELT purposes. However, CCELD was the first dictionary to give detailed accounts of common words which prioritized the uses observed in data, even where the resulting entries seemed counter-intuitive, for example because of sense ordering. Cobuild's success here can be demonstrated by the fact that other dictionaries now do the same. Where CCELD failed was that its long entries were sometimes difficult for users to navigate and locate the information needed[5]: in response, other post-corpus dictionaries developed signposting techniques to simplify such complex cases.

7. Aftermath and beyond

Sinclair's contribution to lexicography, then, can be seen in terms of CCELD and evaluated in terms of the success of that dictionary. Lexicographical practice, as signalled in his 1983 EURALEX address, was reconsidered and new principles developed, leading to major changes in dictionary concept and design. Not all CCELD's features were imitated: some were ignored, some rejected outright. Nevertheless, Sinclair, through CCELD, had a catalytic effect on lexicography, beginning with monolingual learners' dictionaries then spreading to bilingual dictionaries and monolingual dictionaries for adult or child native speakers, in Britain and internationally. It is generally accepted that the Cobuild project blazed the trail with respect to a new methodology and approach, and a new reflexivity and attitude towards the text. See, for example, comments concerning Cobuild in the seminal overviews by Cowie and Landau of respectively EFL lexicography and dictionary-making in general. Both contextualize Cobuild in relation to computational developments in linguistics and lexicography generally, and both make a number of criticisms, yet attest the significance of its achievement:

> Since the publication of *Cobuild 1*, in 1987, the theory and methodology which gave rise to it have had a considerable impact on the development of EFL lexicography… Another result, deeper and more pervasive has been to transform the view which many EFL lexicographers take of the data on which their accounts of meaning and structure are based. (Cowie 1999:128)

> *Cobuild ELD*'s [commitment to the principles of corpus linguistics] was genuine. It was betting the farm on the use of authentic language to inform its research and to furnish its definers with examples. As the reader will see below, I am somewhat critical of the insistence of the *Cobuild* editors on using only authentic examples without alteration, but I do admire their integrity and am certain that they have advanced the discipline of lexicography in no small way.   (Landau 2001:287)

Would lexicography have changed if Cobuild had not existed? Almost certainly: it is likely that corpora would have come into widespread use in any case, and many other changes in learners' dictionaries have happened independently. However, it is pointless to speculate how: better to observe that even a rejection of some of Cobuild's principles and orthodoxies is a measure of Cobuild's influence that they were considered at all, and to observe too that Cobuild's influence spread not only through the dictionary text, or proselytizing by Sinclair, Hanks, and other members of the Cobuild team, but also by cultural transmission through the mobility of the lexicographical work force, with career lexicographers moving between publishers and projects, and ideas disseminating accordingly.

Sinclair's two EURALEX keynote addresses form an interesting pair, not just for the convenient signalling in 1983 of lexicographical practices to be reconsidered and his comments in 2004 on their implementation in Cobuild dictionaries. In 1983, he had drawn attention to the absence of a viable lexicographical theory; his 2004 address, as published, points towards a theory of meaning which dictionaries themselves can instantiate. Such a theory would be driven by what had been learned from corpora (cf. "some startling new concepts will emerge from the interaction between Computational Linguistics and Lexicography" (1984a:11–12)): in particular, that meaning is not word-based but created through longer stretches of text, including multi-word strings and patterns; that texts are not ambiguous and so words cannot be seen as polysemous; and that there is no division between lexical/content words and grammatical/function words, while meaning is created through their interaction. Sinclair (2004b:9) comments: "The theory of meaning takes as its starting point that meaning is holistic, unique to the text in which it appears and unique to each individual participant in the communicative process". Communication succeeds because participants achieve common ground. Sinclair continues:

> It is one of the main jobs of language description to pursue the common ground of meaning as far as it can be taken. Another major job is to reconcile each unique cotext with the language system as a whole; to recognise those aspects of meaning which arise from recurrent patterns like lexical items and to interpret the other patterns which are the result of the juxtapositions and fine tuning of the lexical items. Lexicographers do this all the time... (2004b:9)

While the implication here is that lexicographers and their dictionaries have a major role to fulfil in realizing a theory of meaning, the communicative context — a lexicography conference — has to be taken into account. (Compare, for example, a comment from an address by Sinclair at a conference of semanticists:

> A dictionary is a practical tool, and no place to introduce a new theory of meaning, even if one had been available. So the first dictionary derived from a corpus...

was conservative in its design, in relation to the disturbing nature of the evidence encountered by the lexicographers. (2004a:133)

where the published paper goes on to explore issues relating to the notion of the lexical item, meaning in relation to text, and the problematic nature of existing lexicographical descriptions.)

Can, however, dictionaries go much further in implementing a text-driven theory of meaning, where word meaning is replaced by meaning derived from longer stretches? It is difficult to see how, given the existing state of the art, the constraints of the printed page and alphabetical accessing, and the consequent constraints of electronic dictionaries which are typically still derived from print counterparts. The word, after all, is a convenient linguistic unit, and longer strings have generally proved less tractable to describe and more diffuse — though this again veers into speculation, and lexicography is a broader activity than the production of dictionaries.

Collins' first learner's dictionary in 1974 defined *lexicographer* as 'person who makes a dictionary': very like the definition in Hornby et al's 1948 dictionary for Oxford (*A Learner's Dictionary of Current English*) as 'one who makes a dictionary'. The second edition of CCELD in 1995 treated *lexicographer* as an undefined derivative of *lexicography*, but gave the somewhat deontic example

> A lexicographer's job is to describe the language.

In this shift can be seen something of a particular contribution of Sinclair to lexicography through the Cobuild project: the fact that lexicographical method can be seen as a realistic means of moving towards an understanding and theory of lexis — even meaning — with lexicography a respectable part of linguistics (albeit applied). The real excitement, though, of what the Cobuild project did is better demonstrated by the example which CCELD itself had in 1987:

> Lexicographers are daily discovering new facts about words.

Yet these two examples encapsulate both the strengths and weakness of Cobuild. The strengths, the great contribution, are in terms of the re-evaluation of lexis and the working of language, using a pioneering methodology and (for the time) an advanced technology: Cobuild was a project 'in lexical computing'. The weakness is that Cobuild did not recognize fully enough that CCELD could not be synonymous with Cobuild, and that in producing that first dictionary, it had to do more than describe the language: consequently it neglected the needs of the receiver of the description, the dictionary-user. CCELD was and is magnificent, though it is not unflawed.[6]

When John gave his keynote at the 2004 Euralex congress, I'd expected to hear him look back at the achievements of the Cobuild project, particularly in the 1980s when he was most involved in everyday lexicography, when the radical, innovative lexicographical work was evolving, and the 'disturbing nature' of corpus evidence increasingly apparent. He did, but he also did something more interesting and very typical: he looked forward to where dictionaries could go, to the implications for a new model of the lexicon, that new theory of meaning. In an email commenting on my draft paper, John qualified what I had said about Cobuild's 'relative lack of financial success' and flaws, or limitations on lexicographical developments. He talked of how Cobuild 'could have swept the board; not perhaps the first edition, which was deliberately purist and was there as a marker; [...] but a third that [...] made perhaps sweeping changes — that could have worked'. He did not specify those changes, but it is unlikely that they would have involved backtracking: they would have been still more radical and innovative, more disturbing of the status quo. CCELD itself remains a testimony to John's vision.

Notes

1. Cobuild was a joint project between the University of Birmingham and Collins Publishers (later HarperCollins), funded by Collins and based within the Department of English and headed by John Sinclair. Cobuild is an acronym formed from COllins Birmingham University International Language Database. See Sinclair (1987) for a detailed account of the project and CCELD itself, and Clear et al (1996) for an account of later developments.

2. See Cowie (1999) for a history of monolingual dictionaries for learners, and see Rundell (1998) for an overview of the state of the art in the 1990s.

3. Explanations here are taken from CCELD.

4. Examples are taken from CCELD.

5. See Bogaards (1998) for a discussion of the navigability of four learners' dictionaries.

6. I am indebted to John Sinclair and to Gwyneth Fox for their helpful comments on this paper.

References

Dictionaries

A Learner's Dictionary of Current English. (1948, ed. 1). Later editions published as *The Advanced Learner's Dictionary of Current English* (1965, ed. 2), and *Oxford Advanced Learner's Dictionary of Current English* (1974, ed. 3; 1995, ed. 4). Oxford: Oxford University Press.

Collins Cobuild English Language Dictionary. (1987). London & Glasgow: Collins. Second edition published as *Collins Cobuild English Dictionary* (1995), London & Glasgow: Harper-Collins.

Collins English Learner's Dictionary. (1974). London & Glasgow: Collins.

Idiomatic and Syntactic English Dictionary. (1942). Tokyo: Kaitakusha.

Longman Dictionary of Contemporary English. (1978, ed. 1; 1987, ed. 2; 1995, ed. 3). Harlow: Longman.

Macmillan English Dictionary. (2002). Oxford: Macmillan.

Picture Dictionary. (1967). Burke: London.

Other references

Barnbrook, G. (2002). *Defining Language: A Local Grammar of Definition Sentences*. Amsterdam: John Benjamins.

Bogaards, P. (1998). Scanning long entries in learner's dictionaries. In T. Fontenelle et al (Eds.), *Actes EURALEX '98 Proceedings* (pp. 555–563). Liège: Université de Liège.

Bogaards, P. (1996). Dictionaries for learners of English. *International Journal of Lexicography*, 9 (4), 277–320.

Clear, J., Fox, G., Francis, G., Krishnamurthy, R. & Moon, R. (1996). COBUILD: the state of the art. *International Journal of Corpus Linguistics*, 1 (2), 303–314.

Cowie, A. P. (1999). *English Dictionaries for Foreign Learners*. Oxford: Oxford University Press.

Fox, G. (1987). The case for examples. In J. M. Sinclair (Ed.), *Looking Up: An Account of the CO-BUILD Project in Lexical Computing* (pp. 137–149). London & Glasgow: Collins.

Halliday, M. A. K. & Hasan, R. (1976). *Cohesion in English*. London: Longman.

Hanks, P. (1987). Definitions and explanations. In J. M. Sinclair (Ed.), *Looking Up: An Account of the COBUILD Project in Lexical Computing* (pp. 116–136). London & Glasgow: Collins.

Herbst, T. (1996). On the way to the perfect learners' dictionary: a first comparison of OALD5, LDOCE3, COBUILD2 and CIDE. *International Journal of Lexicography*, 9 (4), 320–358.

Herbst, T. & Popp, K. (Eds.) (1999). *The Perfect Learners' Dictionary?* (Lexicographica Series Maior, Vol. 95). Tübingen: Niemeyer.

Hindmarsh, R. (1980). *Cambridge English Lexicon*. Cambridge: Cambridge University Press.

Hunston, S. & Francis, G. (2000). *Pattern Grammar: A Corpus-driven Approach to the Lexical Grammar of English*. Amsterdam: John Benjamins.

Landau, S. I. (2001) (ed. 2). *Dictionaries: the Art and Craft of Lexicography*. Cambridge: Cambridge University Press.

Rundell, M. (1998). Recent trends in English pedagogical lexicography. *International Journal of Lexicography*, 11 (4), 315–342.

Sinclair, J. M. (2004a). *Trust the Text: Language, Corpus and Discourse*. London: Routledge.

Sinclair, J. M. (2004b). In praise of the dictionary. In G. Williams & S. Vessier (Eds.), *Proceedings of the Eleventh EURALEX Congress, EURALEX 2004* (pp. 1–11). Lorient: Université de Bretagne-Sud.

Sinclair, J. M. (1991). *Corpus, Concordance, Collocation*. Oxford: Oxford University Press.

Sinclair, J. M. (Ed.) (1987). *Looking Up: An Account of the COBUILD Project in Lexical Computing*. London & Glasgow: Collins.

Sinclair, J. M. (1985). Lexicographic evidence. In R. Ilson (Ed.), *Dictionaries, Lexicography, and Language Learning.* Oxford: Pergamon & British Council.

Sinclair, J. M. (1984a). Lexicography as an academic subject. In R. R. K. Hartmann (Ed.), *LEXeter '83 Proceedings* (pp. 3–12). Tübingen: Niemeyer.

Sinclair, J. M. (1984b). Naturalness in language. In J. Aarts & W. Meijs (Eds.), *Corpus Linguistics: Recent Developments in the Use of Computer Corpora in English Language Research* (pp. 203–210). Amsterdam: Rodopi.

West, M. (1953). *A General Service List of English Words.* London: Longmans. (First published 1936 as Part V, *The General Service List, of the Interim Report on Vocabulary Selection*)

Sinclair on collocation

Geoff Barnbrook
University of Birmingham

This paper reassesses the description of collocation given by Sinclair in Chapter 8 of *Corpus, Concordance, Collocation*, in particular the implications of this description for models of language production and interpretation, contrasting the open-choice and idiom principles. The concepts of independent and dependent meanings are explored, along with the relationship between texts and grammar. The arguments put forward in the Chapter are evaluated against collocation evidence obtained from a large reference corpus.

Keywords: collocation, idiom, meaning, grammar, corpus

1. Introduction — a summary of Chapter 8

The Introduction to Chapter 8 of *Corpus, Concordance, Collocation* (Sinclair 1991:109–121 — first published in 1987) states that it "concludes the description of word co-occurrence as we currently conceive it" (Sinclair 1991:109), and refers back to two particular themes dealt with throughout the book: dependent and independent meaning, and the relation of texts to grammar. The chapter is titled 'Collocation', and provides a brief summary of the role played by word co-occurrence in the interpretation of texts.

This role is related to two opposed models of interpretation — the open-choice and idiom principles. The open-choice (or 'slot-and-filler') model, designated as "probably the normal way of seeing and describing language" (1991:109) is seen as placing minimal — basically syntactic — constraints on the choice of lexical items to fill each vacancy arising in the text, and is characterised as the basis of most grammars. In contrast, the idiom principle presupposes that language users select from a set of semi-preconstructed phrases. The role of collocation is then considered within the framework of the two principles of interpretation and Sinclair's original conclusions are evaluated using evidence from dictionaries and collocation data relating to the word *back*.

As a starting-point for discussion of this chapter the nature of the open-choice and idiom principles will now be explored.

2. The open-choice principle

Grammatical models of language tend to separate the lexical and semantic aspects of words from the organisation of syntax, so that sentence structures can be envisaged as sequences of functional slots available for filling by lexical items selected from appropriate subsets of the vocabulary based on part of speech features. As an example, the phrase structure component of Chomsky's transformational grammar provides a set of rules which will generate sentences considered to be grammatical. A simple example of this is provided by Malmkjær (1991:483, adapted from Chomsky (1957)):

Sentence → NP + VP
NP → T + N + Number
Number → {sing, pl}
VP → Verb + NP
Verb → Aux + V
Aux → Tense
Tense → {pres, past}
T → the
N → man, ball, etc.
V → hit, took, etc.

This set of rules ignores all lexical and semantic considerations, although even in this approach such restrictions as transitivity and limited semantic selectivity have had to be acknowledged. The approach also works top down, from the slots or functions assumed to be available within the structures under analysis to the fillers, the classes of lexical components fulfilling those roles.

3. The idiom principle

While the basic units of the open-choice model are individual words, combinable within grammatical constraints, the idiom principle relates to phrases, partly prefabricated multi-word units of indeterminate extent. These phrases can exhibit significant internal variation, both lexical and syntactic, and strong collocation with other words or phrases, or a pattern of co-occurrence with grammatical choices or semantic environments. These semi-preconstructed phrases then constitute single choices, and do not benefit from further grammatical analysis.

4.   The relationship between the principles

Sinclair stresses the non-random nature of language in his consideration of the need for the idiom principle:

> It is clear that words do not occur at random in a text, and that the open-choice principle does not provide for substantial enough restraints on consecutive choices. We would not produce normal text simply by operating the open-choice principle.   (Sinclair 1991:110)

He goes on to point out that even the "large-scale conditioning choices" represented by register, which massively reduce or even pre-empt the open choices, still leave the language model excessive opportunity for choice: "the principle of idiom is put forward to account for the restraints that are not captured by the open-choice model" (Sinclair 1991:110). The idiom principle is therefore suggested because of the inadequacy of the open-choice principle to account for meaning in language. It is, says Sinclair (1991:112), "at least as important as grammar in the explanation of how meaning arises in text". The evidence for this claim is based on the features of the idiom principle noted above, especially the nature and extent of patterns of co-occurrence — collocation between words and phrases and their co-occurrence with particular grammatical structures and within particular semantic environments. The next section examines the claims made in detail.

5.   Claims made for the idiom principle

In Chapter 8 Sinclair lists some features of the idiom principle which, he claims, show that it "is far more pervasive and elusive than we have allowed so far" (Sinclair 1991:111). Moon (1998:2–5) discusses the terminological problems presented by the range of meanings of the word 'idiom' in English and uses the term 'fixed expression' to cover a whole set of linguistic phenomena: "several kinds of phrasal lexeme, phraseological unit, or multi-word lexical item" (Moon 1998:2). The relevant characteristics exhibited by phrases which behave in similar ways to those units of meaning already seen as idiomatic can be summarised as follows:

a.   indeterminate extent
b.   internal lexical variation
c.   internal syntactic variation
d.   variation in word order
e.   strong collocational attraction for other words
f.   co-occurrence with certain grammatical structures
g.   tendency to occur in certain semantic environments

These features allow the idiom principle to be extended far beyond the "fairly triv-ial mismatch between the writing system and the grammar" (Sinclair 1991:110) which allows phrases to maintain their 'structurally bogus' word spaces despite their coalescence into single units of meaning, and even beyond the collection of phrases conventionally seen as idiomatic. Sinclair's condition for this treatment encompasses "any occasion where one decision leads to more than one word in text" (Sinclair 1991:111). Features a) to d) allow phrases to vary significantly while still being considered as subject to the idiom principle, while e) to g) lead to re-strictions of independent choice rather than a complete set of constraints.

This may seem at first sight to relax the requirements for treatment as an idiom too far, but it should be remembered that the original claim is that there are re-strictions on choice which go beyond those of grammar and register: even the ten-dencies toward simultaneous choice of more than one word, represented by some degree of fixity in the structure of a phrase or a strong collocational, syntactic or semantic patterning associated with a word or phrase, form significant restrictions on the open-choice principle. Sinclair's claim is that:

> ...the overwhelming nature of this evidence leads us to elevate the principle of idiom from being a rather minor feature, compared with grammar, to being at least as important as grammar in the explanation of how meaning arises in text.
>
> (Sinclair 1991:112)

Moon (1998:30) discusses language acquisition research which "suggests that lan-guage is learned, stored, retrieved and produced in holophrases and multi-word items". The textual evidence called in support of Sinclair's claim is considered in the next section.

6. Texts, meaning and grammar

Sinclair documents a series of 'problems' which have arisen during the lexical anal-ysis of long texts carried out during the 1980s in the first large scale corpus lin-guistic investigations, most notably in the Cobuild dictionary project (described in detail in Sinclair (1987), and cf. Moon's paper, this volume). These problems re-late generally to the meanings of frequently occurring words: in some cases these words seem to have very little meaning, and the most frequent meanings of the most frequent words (and even of some of the less frequent words) are not usu-ally "the meanings supplied by introspection" (Sinclair 1991:112). Sinclair uses the word *back* as an example here, showing that the meaning generally given first place in dictionaries is actually relatively uncommon in large corpora. The tendency for more frequent words to exhibit less clear and independent meanings, which can often only be explained in terms of usage, is seen as an important correlate of the idiom principle, leading to fewer choices of larger linguistic units being made in normal language use. Since normal text is made up of the largely delexicalised frequent words and more frequent senses of less frequent words, it becomes itself largely delexicalised, and relatively impervious to grammatical analysis to the extent that it is constructed on the idiom principle. On this basis:

> A model of language which divides grammar and lexis, and which uses the grammar to provide a string of lexical choice points, is a secondary model.

and:

> The open-choice analysis could be imagined as an analytical process which goes on in principle all the time, but whose results are only intermittently called for.   (both Sinclair 1991:114)

Both of these claims sideline the dominant top-down grammatical model in favour of a bottom-up lexically driven model.

The following two sections assess the evidence relating to the idiom principle from grammars and dictionaries, while Section 9 examines Sinclair's summary of the role of collocation and evaluates it against evidence from the corpus.

7.   Evidence from grammars

While mainstream grammars have already been characterised both in the chapter and in this evaluation as top-down open-choice models with inadequate restraints on the choice of items in text, they have developed in response to criticisms similar to those put in the chapter. Head-driven phrase-structure grammar (HPSG) now takes into account lexical and semantic features in addition to purely syntactic criteria; Optimality Theory seems to provide a basis for syntactic constraints to be less significant than others, perhaps based on the idiom principle. More specialised grammars reflect the need for the constraints imposed by the idiom principle more explicitly: in particular pattern grammars and local grammars related to functional subsets of language.

The first pattern grammar published by Cobuild deals with verbs (Francis, Hunston & Manning 1996). In its introduction it states that it "presents all the patterns of English verbs, and relates these patterns to both structure and meaning" (p. vii). In the general account of the production of the pattern grammars (Hunston & Francis 2000) the aim of the series is described:

> ...to show all the patterns of all the lexical items in the Collins COBUILD Eng-
> lish Dictionary, and within each to show all the lexical items that have that pat-
> tern.   (Hunston & Francis 2000:35)

This approach to a description of the syntactic behaviour of lexis involves a reor-
ganisation of the grammar information contained within the dictionary, but the
resulting set of grammar patterns is firmly based on the properties of the lexical
items listed rather than on a top-down hierarchy of syntactic slots to be filled.

The local grammar approach is even more directly influenced by the idiom
principle. Originally proposed by Gross (in, for example, the 1993 publication listed in the references) to deal with specialised forms of text structure found within
normal text, the concept has been applied, among other areas, to definition sentences (Barnbrook 2002), evaluation (Hunston & Sinclair 2000), causation (Allen
2005) and the identification of proper names (Traboulsi 2004). In each case the
grammar is based on recurrent structures related to the communicative function
of the piece of text under consideration, which restrict the freedom of combination of linguistic units in a similar way to that proposed by the idiom principle. In
the case of the definition sentence grammar described in Barnbrook (2002), only
17 basic structural types were needed to describe the complete set of over 31,000
definition sentences within a published dictionary. Each of these types represents
a combination of phrases within the description of the idiom principle.

8.   Evidence from dictionaries — dependent and independent meaning

Dictionaries classically treat words as being both capable and worthy of treatment
as independent units of language in parallel with their possible discussion as ag-
glomerates of morphemes and as components of phrases. As an example, consider
the treatment of *back* in the *Merriam-Webster Online Dictionary* (2005)[1]:

> Main Entry: **back**
> Function: *noun*
> Etymology: Middle English, from Old English *bæc;* akin to Old High German *bah*
> back
> **1 a** (1) : the rear part of the human body especially from the neck to the end of
> the spine (2) : the body considered as the wearer of clothes (3) : capacity for labor,
> effort, or endurance (4) : the back considered as the seat of one's awareness of duty
> or failings <get off my *back*> **b** : the part of a lower animal (as a quadruped) cor-
> responding to the human back **c** : SPINAL COLUMN **d**: BACKBONE 4
> **2 a** : the side or surface opposite the front or face : the rear part; *also* : the farther
> or reverse side **b** : something at or on the back for support <*back* of a chair> **c** : a
> place away from the front <sat in *back*>

3 : a position in some games (as football or soccer) behind the front line of players;
also : a player in this position
- **backed** *adjective*
- **back·less** *adjective*
- **back of one's hand** *or* **back of the hand** : a show of contempt
- **back of one's mind** : the remote part of one's mind where thoughts and memories are stored to be drawn on
- **behind one's back** : without one's knowledge : in secret
- **in back of** : <u>BEHIND</u>

To aid navigation through the entries given on the website for *back* a selection screen is provided which lists the ten senses made available through the free online version of this dictionary. The first four senses given for *back* relate to the single word together with its part of speech (in the sequence noun, adverb, adjective and verb), followed by a capitalised fifth sense (*Back*, the name of a Canadian river) and five phrasal senses (*back-and-forth, back and forth, back away, back bacon* and *back burner*). The entry for the last of these phrasal senses is:

> Main Entry: **back burner**
> Function: *noun*
> : the condition of being out of active consideration or development — usually used in the phrase *on the back burner*

This treatment of the word, selected because of Sinclair's use of it in Chapter 8 as an illustration, shows the dominance of independent meaning for the lexicographers in this case. The primary meanings relate to individual word senses of *back* considered through part of speech classification rather than any semantic, context-dependent features, and the phrasal meanings are effectively treated as single units dependent only on the other elements of the phrase for their consideration.

This approach to the definition and description of words in dictionaries has been challenged, especially, during the last two decades, by the Cobuild range of dictionaries produced under the original supervision of Sinclair (see also Moon's paper, this volume). The Cobuild range adopted a full sentence definition form which provided much of the context necessary for the meaning of the word in use in the language, dependent on its environment, to be properly appreciated. As an example, consider the definition of sense ① of *back* in the *Collins COBUILD English Dictionary for Advanced Learners* (2001) (*CCED*):

> If you move **back**, you move in the opposite direction to the one in which you are facing or in which you were moving before.

In the case of this word, which has a very large number of senses, the dictionary is organised initially into three main groups, corresponding generally to adverbial, noun and adjective and verb uses. General phrasal uses are dealt with within these categories, while established phrasal verbs are dealt with under separate headwords. Within each group senses are dealt with in a sequence which reflects the relative frequency of the dependent meaning under consideration.

Similar organisational approaches have now been adopted by many other dictionaries, especially those produced for non-native learners of English. As an example, the *Cambridge Advanced Learners' Dictionary* (2005) produces a very large (189 items) selection list when *back* is entered as a search term. The first ten items in this list are given below:

> back (RETURN)
> back (FURTHER AWAY)
> back (FURTHEST PART)
> back (SUPPORT)
> back (BODY PART)
> back (SPORT)
> backchat
> backup
> back copy
> back door

In each of the 189 entries in this list the context on which the meaning of the word depends is used to distinguish the different senses that the user might want to consult. This approach recognises that meaning, far from being an independent characteristic of the word form itself, depends crucially on the context of use of the word.

The adoption of the idiom principle in the organisation of dictionaries aimed at learners of English is particularly significant: such dictionaries provide the learners' only guidance on the behaviour of English lexis and need to be organized in the clearest and most efficient way possible; dictionaries intended for native speakers represent only one rather specialised source of information on the more obscure areas of English lexis, and the uses to which they are put are in general less clear and less well defined.

Sinclair suggests at the beginning of Chapter 8 (1991:109) that a dictionary of collocations should be produced. Such dictionaries do now exist: the *Oxford Collocations Dictionary for Students of English* (2002) (OCDSE), for example. The website advertising this dictionary claims in the discussion of its key features:

> Collocations — common word combinations such as 'bright idea' or 'talk freely' — are the essential building blocks of natural-sounding English. The dictionary contains over 150,000 collocations for nearly 9,000 headwords.

> The dictionary shows all the words that are commonly used in combination with each headword: nouns, verbs, adjectives, adverbs, and prepositions as well as common phrases.
>
> (http://www.oup.com/elt/catalogue/isbn/0-19-431243-7?cc=global)

In the introduction to the dictionary collocation is described as "the way words combine in a language to produce natural-sounding speech and writing" (p.vii), a description which seems to reflect very closely that of the idiom principle in general. The introduction goes on to make the link absolutely explicit "Combinations of words in a language can be ranged on a cline from the totally free… to the totally fixed and idiomatic." It also stresses the ubiquity of collocation: "No piece of natural spoken or written English is totally free of collocation".

The dictionary's treatment of the headword *back* is found on p. 50. OCDSE only provides entries for noun, verb and adjective senses of headwords. In the case of *back* only two noun senses are dealt with (part of the body and part furthest from the front), two verb senses (move backwards, support) and one phrasal verb sense (for *back down*). While the dictionary provides useful collocation information for the more strongly lexical uses of the word (Sinclair's 'meanings supplied by introspection' (1991:112)), it ignores the much more frequent delexicalised meanings of frequent words.

9.   Collocation and the evidence from the corpus

Finally in Chapter 8, Sinclair examines the phenomenon of collocation, which "illustrates the idiom principle" (1991:115). This is an interesting choice of words: collocation does not simply provide evidence for the operation of the idiom principle, but is a manifestation of that operation. He formulates a distinction between upward and downward collocation, relationships between collocates of unequal overall frequencies in the corpus, and at the end of the chapter (1991:116–121) provides the results of an investigation of collocates of the word *back* which shows the main features of the analysis in operation. The data also shows the distinction between upward and downward collocation in operation. This investigation has now been carried out again using the 450 million word corpus of the Bank of English.

In the first place, a sample of 100 of the more than 440,000 concordance lines for *back* from the corpus was examined to estimate the distribution of senses on the basis of the definitions given in CCED (2001:97–8). Of this sample, 70 belonged to the mainly adverbial senses grouped under main entry 1, 18 to the noun and adjective senses under main entry 2, and 2 to the verb senses under main entry 3. 10 of them represented senses dealt with elsewhere in the dictionary under phrases based on other headwords. These results bear out the comments made by Sinclair on the evidence provided on meanings by long texts, already referred to in Section 6. In the vast majority of the sample concordance lines the meaning of *back* represented belongs to the largely delexicalised range predicted by the idiom principle.

His comments on collocation have also been evaluated against the evidence provided by the Bank of English. Sinclair's original list of collocates of *back* is avowedly provisional and uses only ad hoc groups rather than any organised separation into senses (1991:116). Upward and downward collocates are separated on the basis of frequency: the original definition allocates collocates whose frequency is within 15% of the node word's frequency to a buffer zone of neutrality, though these are reallocated in the later classified lists. The Appendix shows lists of collocates of *back* from the 450 million word Bank of English, ordered by *t*-score and classified into upward and downward collocates. In the case of words which belong to a multiform lemma a further classification has been made: in some cases individual word forms constitute downward collocates while the lemma as a whole forms an upward collocate, and these have been appropriately noted. All upward collocates (both individual and on lemmatisation) are shown, together with the top 120 downward collocates.

From this list it can be seen that the upward collocate list resembles very closely that produced by Sinclair, especially when the lemmatised list is taken into account for verb forms. The list of downward collocates is much more extensive than in the original chapter, but the further collocates found confirm the general core meanings and associated syntactic patterns suggested by Sinclair's original results. Throughout the most significant collocates there is the preponderance of past tenses noted by Sinclair (1991:119), such as *was, came, went* and *took* in the upward collocates, and *brought, turned, pulled, sent* and *looked* towards the top of the downward list.

10. Conclusion

The evidence from the Bank of English confirms the evidence originally provided by Sinclair for *back*, and provides strong evidence for the idiom principle as a basis of interpretation of text. Language does not seem to operate on the basis of syntactic slots available for filling with minimal structural restrictions, but instead largely on the basis of preconstructed phrases composed largely of delexicalised frequent words. This means in turn that the principles of general grammar are rather less important than the behavioural patterns of lexical items, specifically those revealed by an analysis of collocation. If the idiom principle can operate as the main basis for interpretation of texts, there are clear implications for the modes of production of texts, not explicitly pursued in Sinclair's chapter, which would repay further investigation.

The significance of collocation is now generally recognised, but the mechanics of its analysis still lag behind the potential identified by John. Advances in analysis techniques were largely driven by his refusal to accept the limitations that data processing imposed at any given time, and we need to keep up the level of the demands that he continually made on the data and on the algorithms used to investigate it. It is a much harder task without his direct inspiration, but it is essential if we are to understand the processes of language.

Note

1. Some features of this dictionary, such as links to pronunciation examples and phonetic transcriptions, have been omitted.

References

Allen, C. M. (2005). *A local grammar of cause and effect: a corpus-driven study*. Unpublished PhD Thesis. Birmingham: University of Birmingham.

Barnbrook G. (2002). *Defining Language: A Local Grammar of Definition Sentences*. Amsterdam: John Benjamins Publishers.

Cambridge Advanced Learner's Dictionary. (2005). Consulted at http://dictionary.cambridge.org/

Chomsky, N. (1957). *Syntactic Structures*. The Hague: Mouton.

Collins COBUILD English Dictionary for Advanced Learners. (2001, ed. 3). London & Glasgow: HarperCollins.

Francis, G., Hunston, S., & Manning, E. (1996). *Collins COBUILD Grammar Patterns 1: Verbs*. London: Harper Collins.

Gross, M. (1993). Local grammars and their representation by finite automata. In M. Hoey (Ed.), *Data, Description, Discourse* (pp. 26–38). London: HarperCollins.

Hunston, S. & Francis, G. (2000). *Pattern Grammar: a Corpus-driven Approach to the Lexical Grammar of English* (Studies in Corpus Linguistics 4). Amsterdam: John Benjamins.

Hunston, S. & Sinclair, J. (2000). A local grammar of evaluation. In S. Hunston & G. Thompson (Eds.), *Evaluation in Text: Authorial Stance and the Construction of Discourse* (pp. 75–100). Oxford: Oxford University Press.

Malmkjær, K. (Ed.) (1991). *The Linguistics Encyclopedia*. London: Routledge.

Merriam-Webster Online Dictionary (2005). http://www.merriam-webster.com (accessed 2 November 2005).

Moon, R. (1998). *Fixed Expressions and Idioms in English: a Corpus-Based Approach*. Oxford: Oxford University Press.

Oxford Collocations Dictionary for Students of English. (2002). Oxford: Oxford University Press.

Sinclair, J. M. (1991). *Corpus, Concordance, Collocation*. Oxford: Oxford University Press. (Chapter 8, 'Collocation', was first published in 1987 in R. Steele & T. Threadgold (Eds.), *Language Topics: Essays in Honour of Michael Halliday*, Amsterdam: John Benjamins.)

Sinclair, J. M. (Ed.) (1987). *Looking Up: An Account of the COBUILD Project in Lexical Computing and the Development of the Collins COBUILD English Language Dictionary*. London: Collins ELT.

Sinclair J., Hoelter, M. & Peters, C. (Eds.). (1995). *The Language of Definition: the Formalization of Dictionary Definitions for Natural Language Processing*. Luxembourg: European Commission.

Traboulsi, H. N. (2004). *A Local Grammar for Proper Names*. Thesis submitted for transfer from MPhil to PhD, unpublished, http://portal.surrey.ac.uk/pls/portal/docs/PAGE/COMPUTING/RESEARCH/PG/2004_TRABOULSI_TRANSFER.PDF (accessed 2 Nov. 2005)

Appendix

Collocates of *back* from the 450 million word Bank of English ordered by *t*-score
Total frequency of *back* – 440,805

Upward collocates

Collocate	Freq. in corpus	Freq. as collocate	t-score
to	11,218,716	183,911	223.156919
into	668,885	21,784	111.960432
on	3,154,716	45,783	98.042444
his	1,936,210	31,170	90.31972
i	3,383,437	43,234	79.98311
then	526,948	13,384	79.875314
he	2,853,158	37,874	79.33817
and	10,608,346	106,485	70.708779
her	963,421	16,487	69.405734
the	24,780,121	226,993	67.483959
when	995,221	16,113	65.290488
him	597,098	11,358	62.521291
my	662,989	12,011	62.029011
at	2,331,553	27,154	53.533301
she	1,042,897	14,546	52.616531
we	1,486,402	18,504	50.112113
from	1,920,773	22,292	48.152084

Collocate	Freq. in corpus	Freq. as collocate	t-score
them	652,612	9,434	44.298338
me	514,252	7,973	44.007923
your	601,144	8,765	43.134565
after	681,330	9,575	43.104309
up	1,009,342	12,056	37.520532
you	2,248,154	22,868	34.328533
now	623,816	7,858	33.313201
they	1,830,327	18,230	28.429495
their	1,220,197	12,369	24.949981
in	8,143,020	70,094	22.916016
but	2,120,938	19,710	21.607257
just	601,829	6,424	21.109707
will	1,273,351	11,914	17.424425
years	498,759	5,170	17.361774
it	3,994,942	34,548	16.87503
can	928,243	8,803	16.03436
time	705,993	6,539	12.217038
could	578,616	5,345	10.88038
our	460,178	4,257	9.789356
would	977,594	8,195	5.615783
was	3,246,851	26,366	5.152642

Individually downward collocates, upward collocates as lemmas

Collocate	Freq. in corpus	Freq. as collocate	t-score
go	348,673	17,743	112.621121
come	248,593	16,342	112.545623
get	440,446	16,985	103.753731
came	187,484	10,679	89.074107
went	177,330	7,804	72.556846
going	302,739	7,995	62.793034
coming	82,810	5,153	62.713928
got	276,803	6,501	53.635364
goes	63,210	2,703	42.43078
getting	99,919	2,836	38.501388
comes	81,728	2,193	33.107122
gets	46,234	1,006	20.256052
took	160,283	2,081	17.991308

Downward collocates

Collocate	Freq. in corpus	Freq. as collocate	t-score
again	208,214	7,370	66.778589
full	145,199	6,130	63.712537
bring	67,629	4,975	62.994683
home	288,830	7,723	62.038584
put	219,706	6,481	59.046224
ll	204,826	6,232	58.542157
way	395,036	8,379	57.604233
brought	77,249	4,054	54.131474
forth	12,073	3,107	54.037442
turned	90,910	4,071	52.601288
look	190,797	4,788	47.514761
seat	28,358	2,623	46.861581
hit	82,680	3,288	46.003731
looking	115,865	3,606	44.878898
door	63,835	2,915	44.694299
pulled	26,967	2,341	44.001511
head	142,147	3,617	41.557441
down	368,341	6,154	41.528561
cut	94,279	2,976	40.964098
sent	67,983	2,610	40.625136
laid	19,613	1,921	40.310715
turn	91,602	2,820	39.540617
straight	44,194	2,164	39.048965
sit	32,853	1,937	38.142048
injury	35,665	1,957	37.898946
looked	90,340	2,666	37.876215
bounce	4,435	1,451	37.176539
room	116,657	2,859	36.315007
fight	46,287	1,933	35.687995
front	100,674	2,615	35.657511
fought	15,481	1,500	35.586934
row	27,087	1,664	35.571064
bounced	3,384	1,227	34.268959
dating	6,218	1,259	34.104499
track	38,517	1,714	34.085317
neck	17,463	1,395	33.673416
chair	21,058	1,435	33.51052
centre	97,321	2,331	32.431041
behind	104,456	2,403	32.265821

Collocate	Freq. in corpus	Freq. as collocate	t-score
right	361,303	5,146	32.133928
ball	69,119	1,951	31.866137
car	116,419	2,487	31.514462
hold	61,335	1,817	31.312495
pushed	18,250	1,245	31.217734
turning	28,724	1,386	31.16249
bringing	20,909	1,255	30.785225
pull	21,047	1,220	30.190582
sat	37,671	1,434	30.046339
england	140,636	2,639	29.845664
take	306,798	4,376	29.685101
send	44,879	1,494	29.522838
holding	34,891	1,362	29.471636
soon	85,884	1,984	29.381439
basics	3,071	902	29.229319
dates	11,430	982	28.468955
walked	26,432	1,171	28.146522
step	46,464	1,416	27.921053
held	96,478	2,010	27.91275
gone	71,979	1,706	27.601454
together	117,920	2,228	27.558732
left	209,289	3,197	27.438051
yard	17,079	999	27.358254
pain	33,238	1,208	27.236975
want	255,528	3,641	27.043686
wing	26,217	1,093	26.825356
money	192,027	2,964	26.709409
hair	48,472	1,360	26.54346
fall	55,088	1,406	25.945084
brings	15,816	902	25.892646
moved	58,514	1,441	25.840441
memories	13,781	865	25.726626
towards	69,128	1,549	25.546964
later	158,106	2,523	25.479949
welcome	26,303	1,018	25.42412
before	385,939	4,771	25.139403
cutting	21,847	936	24.979359
normal	38,925	1,153	24.942403
work	323,761	4,139	24.766163
leaned	3,915	668	24.654672

Collocate	Freq. in corpus	Freq. as collocate	t-score
garden	49,214	1,263	24.65031
mind	90,086	1,696	23.982795
win	125,627	2,082	23.98084
clock	19,472	847	23.842535
let	127,545	2,091	23.796195
onto	21,671	864	23.596932
envelope	5,560	641	23.591254
buy	76,387	1,518	23.54591
forward	65,169	1,389	23.520419
traced	3,203	586	23.167073
foot	37,750	1,037	22.985164
stepped	12,213	697	22.763424
haunt	2,295	551	22.704641
move	101,541	1,740	22.573219
knocked	10,420	662	22.545047
half	181,831	2,571	22.508606
across	92,880	1,640	22.463522
hand	120,445	1,934	22.442624
handed	21,217	796	22.300517
shot	62,615	1,291	22.228223
drove	15,800	717	22.137319
tears	14,735	693	21.923799
never	247,311	3,180	21.908333
earth	41,535	1,023	21.773718
headed	21,858	777	21.709096
flew	11,935	636	21.497943
feet	44,554	1,044	21.468885
forced	46,269	1,064	21.465892
pay	117,915	1,849	21.438562
fell	48,303	1,071	21.120833
fighting	38,692	948	20.908762
claw	1,364	457	20.875871
hotel	51,772	1,090	20.685269
heading	14,115	629	20.654675
d	321,089	3,792	20.580677
us	414,159	4,659	20.548136
flat	34,374	876	20.465523
pulling	10,151	566	20.435869
legs	21,012	700	20.213044
off	382,376	4,337	20.202512
push	20,546	692	20.164719

Notes on the ofness of *of* — Sinclair and grammar

Charles Owen
University of Birmingham

Sinclair's grammatical work is notable for its strict reliance on performance data and its avoidance of psychological theorising. His argument rests on the observation that large corpora reveal a huge discrepancy between the predictions made by cognitive models of grammar and what actually happens in performance. This discrepancy cannot be explained away by appeal to encoding/processing deficiencies, but must be taken as reason to revise our view of grammar, especially by exploring its interdependence with lexis. In this he follows Halliday's (1966) idea that every word has its own grammar. Sinclair's 1991 paper on the word *of* ('The meeting of lexis and grammar') exemplifies his thinking in this area with particular energy and originality. Questioning the traditional classification of *of* as a preposition, he proposes a new, more semantically based, approach to the analysis of noun phrases traditionally said to contain postmodification of the head with an *of*-phrase, e.g. *the horns of the bull*. This chapter reviews Sinclair's development as a grammarian, examines the arguments of the 1991 paper and suggests that while his work has been radically transformative in linguistics, it should not indefinitely avoid engaging with the problem of how best to represent what it is that we know when we say we know a language.

Keywords: lexicogrammar, corpus-based grammatical method, noun phrase structure, functions of *of*

1. Introductory remarks

Grammatical tradition, no matter what turns it has taken, has essentially been a quest for more comprehensive, more economical, more refined, more useful statements of the regularities which seem to characterise human language, i.e. the hierarchically and sequentially ordered categories and patterns which it is supposed speakers of a language in some way know in order to understand and produce messages. We must presume that Sinclair began his career in grammar with the same aims as any other grammarian. What makes him unusual is his stance on the notion of 'regularities', and also on the issue of 'knowledge'. Tradition tends to state regularities in terms of categories and mechanisms such as word class, constituency, dependency, taxis and sequence. Much recent grammatical theory rests explicitly or implicitly on the belief that speakers are aware of these categories and mechanisms, at least subconsciously, and that grammatical statements should reflect that awareness. Sinclair has produced two major grammars (Sinclair 1972, 1990), both of which do deploy many of these traditional concepts. Yet as time went by, and particularly by the time of the article we shall be looking at presently: 'The meeting of lexis and grammar' (Sinclair 1991:81–98), it seems he became increasingly convinced that the really important regularities were not the ones mentioned above but lexical ones, and that knowledge is too imponderable or inaccessible to be bothered with.

In *A Course in Spoken English: Grammar* (1972), there is evidence that he was already uneasy about badness of fit between standard statements of regularities and language performance. It was in fact Part 3 of a series in which Parts 1 and 2 were *Texts, Drills and Tests* (Mackin 1967) and *Intonation* (Halliday 1970). A little unexpectedly in view of the title, the Introduction says that the description "concentrates on the most common varieties of **spoken and written** British English" (my emphasis) but that "there is rather more emphasis on informal spoken English than you commonly find in grammars" (p. 1). A little later we read: "A lot of research is needed before a description of the real structure of speech can be made. But apart from that, the book tries to give many examples of structures that are common in speech" (p.4). Although speech is arguably no more representative of performance than writing, there is more than a hint that previous grammars had misled by failing to capture regularities of spoken performance. "The real structure of speech" is a clear signal of concern that grammar had been dealing with something 'unreal', a contrast later to feature prominently in the branding of Cobuild dictionaries and grammars.

In this early grammar, the word *of* (the subject of the 1991 paper) makes a relatively inconsequential appearance in a section on "rankshift in nominal group structure" (pp. 142–9). It is described and clearly labelled as a preposition introducing qualifying (i.e. postmodifying) structures, as in *the curious behaviour of the man*. Sinclair tells us it is "a bit clumsy and pompous, because the *'s* structure is common in conversation" (p. 145). That is, in conversation we would say *the man's curious behaviour*. Perhaps we would, but the title of the recent bestselling novel *The curious incident of the dog in the night-time* can not, I venture on the basis of introspection, easily be spoken (or written) as: *The dog in the night-time's curious incident.* The reason for this must lie in the different relationship existing in the two examples between the *of*-phrase and the preceding noun. How that relationship should be characterised is what lies at the heart of Sinclair's paper on *of.* Just a year before it appeared, Sinclair had published the second of his two major grammars (Sinclair 1990). As in the 1971 grammar, *of* receives conventional treatment (pp. 129–130). The likely reason is that the 1990 grammar is a mass market product for second-language learners, who are not necessarily the best target for one's most experimental ideas. It is therefore interesting to focus on a point in Sinclair's thinking where he is content for a learner's grammar to say one thing, while deep down he really believes something else. The 1991 paper is truly representative of Sinclair's most stimulating work in grammar, being on the one excitingly creative and energetic, and on the other hand tantalisingly opaque.

2.   Lexicogrammar and the so-called 'Cult of the Counter-example'

It cannot be denied that language performance, once caught, exhibits myriad phenomena which resist the tight embrace of statements of regularities. One standard response is to say, in effect, that 'nobody's perfect': there is a gap between what people know (at some level) and what they do. And why should that surprise us? It is after all typical of the known universe; random failure to conform to regularities may even be what underpins evolution. Unfortunately grammatical modelling of this gap has often been predicated on little more than deficit, buttressed by concepts such as the 'ideal native-speaker', by contrast with whom, it is said, we all perform imperfectly. Presentation of theory can be unhelpful with its talk of rules, principles, parameters and so forth, all suggesting that any unpredicted data will have to be treated either as erroneous (i.e. ungrammatical), or in desperate need of some, any, kind of explanation to permit its incorporation into the description. This seldom leads to wholehearted revision; grammarians are notorious for dodging and tweaking.

This is an approach Sinclair has specifically rejected. His early unease about descriptions developed into a position where the important gap for theory is not one between supposed abstract knowledge and performance, but between descriptions and the 'facts of performance', whether or not they claim to represent knowledge. The extent of this gap is so great that it even calls into question the principle of attempting to represent knowledge. For Sinclair, the mismatch of performance data with explanations of the abstract knowledge base is so glaring that he is much more inclined to dismiss abstract knowledge as an unverifiable construct. As we know, the most startling product of concordancing software is the instant picture it gives of the statistics of language. If we assert that grammar is about regularities, it would seem that there is no more effective way of uncovering these than concordancing; but the regularities which stare out at us from the screen are not always the ones which conventional grammars prepared us for. For Sinclair, the inescapable scientific logic is that a grammar is (or should be) a predictive model of language performance, so where it turns out that there is a large amount of performance which is not predicted, the correct conclusion to draw is that the grammar must be invalid rather than that there is a gap between knowledge and performance.

To illustrate, his 1972 description of *of the man* as a postmodifying prepositional phrase is replaced in 1991 by one in which *man* becomes a second head noun in a double-headed group. Additionally, the idea that speakers know that *the curious behaviour of the man* is related in some way to a clause such as *the man behaves curiously*, or even to the genitive *the man's curious behaviour*, is considered hardly relevant to the understanding of such nominal groups. Stated baldly in this way, this may look to some readers like a minor tweak, but it is deceptive since it impinges on our whole view of grammar.

Let us consider the various ways in which a grammar might be said to have failed to predict performance. Broadly, I think there are three. It might predict performance which does not happen; or it might fail to predict performance which does happen; or, in between these clear cases, it might predict what happens but only at a level of detail which leaves us with further explaining to do. A well-worn example of the first type comes from grammars which predict the occurrence of multiply recursive structures which do not in fact occur, e.g. *The man the dog the car startled bit sued.* The generative grammarian's explanation for their non-occurrence usually invokes 'processing limitations'. There could of course be more convincing explanations involving shared knowledge and the discourse situation of the speaker who wants to convey this information about a man who sues after being bitten by a startled dog. Such explanations would spare the generative grammarian the need to erect a semi-plausible psycholinguistic blocking device, and leave this bit of grammar on embedded clauses not only intact but also integrated into a more comprehensive model of performance. The explanation for non-occurrence would be social rather than psychological. In other words, one does not have to resort to psycho-cognitive explanations for the gap between prediction and performance; it is quite possible to retain an element of grammar such as recursive embedding which predicts non-occurring performance so long as you do not rely exclusively on grammar to predict performance. While Sinclair would probably agree if pressed that, yes, a social rather than a psychological explanation is more credible, this kind of failure actually holds no interest for him. Moreover, he extends this lack of interest to a more general tendency to suppress any interest in rarity. Whereas a lepidopterist would be overjoyed to discover a four-legged moth, and begin to debate whether it actually was a moth, Sinclair loftily dismisses an interest in exceptions as "the cult of the counter-example" (Sinclair 1991:99).

Failure to predict performance which does happen encompasses a much wider range of phenomena — including familiar disfluencies such as anacoluthon, intrusive pronouns in relative clauses and other exotica. Conventional grammar accommodates the 'ungrammatical' performance found in spoken language using a combination of idealisation and other principles of interaction. Sinclair's sense of this kind of failure is of a completely different order of magnitude. When he complains about failure to predict performance, he is not talking about frills like anacoluthon. He is not even necessarily talking about spoken performance. Failure goes right to the very heart of the matter. For example, *of* is one of the most frequent words in the language, contributing to a complex network of grammatical possibilities and meanings. The *Oxford English Dictionary* devotes sixty paragraphs to *of* although it is really a grammatical word, having negligible, if any, intrinsic semantic content in modern English. Every dictionary you pick up will call it a preposition. Sinclair says the equivalent of 'hold on — how can it be?' We shall come to his reasons presently, but meanwhile we should remember that no grammar of any hue can avoid idealisation of some kind. Idealisation is of the essence (a rare use of *of* by the way), since any grammar is a balancing act between capturing regularity and exploring delicacy. Although it is one of Sinclair's most explicit and laudable aims to write grammar which is as exception-proof as possible, his method of dealing with inconvenient examples is subject to the same constraints as any other method. Indeed, when we come to our Sinclairian fragment, we find that he too never quite manages to 'mop up' (as he puts it) all his observed data except by recourse to some very dodgy manoeuvres and the judicious introduction of a dustbin labelled 'miscellaneous'. Where a mentalist says 'this is English because I, a well-informed native-speaker, deem that it is', Sinclair says with equal certitude, 'if this is not in my corpus it is not English, or not proven to be English' or maybe, in frustration, 'this is in my corpus, but it is too infrequent to warrant my close attention'.

Disparaging an interest in rarity as cultish while at the same time claiming to take account of all observable data is an interesting gambit. It could also point to a certain theoretical defensiveness and it is worth dwelling briefly on the cause. Sinclair himself seldom if ever engages directly with his opponents' views on the validity of corpus evidence, but others have taken up the challenge. In an attack on the poverty of stimulus aspect of nativist acquisition theory, Sampson (2005:71 and previous writings) castigates the attitude of nativists to observable data as, for example, "disdainful". Anyone who has worked in Sinclair's shadow for many years might suspect Sampson of exaggeration — surely to goodness those mentalists have looked at corpora by now? — but in fact it is easy to find evidence for the justness of Sampson's critique. Take this short statement from a 2002 textbook aimed at students:

> While corpora are unquestionably invaluable sources of data, they can only be a partial representation of what goes on in the mind. More particularly, corpora will only contain instances of grammatical (or precisely well-formed) sentences (sentences that sound OK to a native speaker). You might think that this would be enough for a linguist to do her job. But corpora are just not enough: there is no way of knowing whether a corpus has *all* the possible forms of grammatical sentences. In fact...due to the infinite and productive nature of language, a corpus could *never* contain all the grammatical forms of a language, nor could it even contain a representative sample.
>
> (Carnie 2002:10)

This betrays limited understanding of what corpora contain; they certainly do not comprise only well-formed sentences for example. But the fatal thrust is in the last few words; fatal, that is, if true. The assertion that the Bank of English or the British National Corpus could never **in principle** be representative of the language denies at a stroke the validity of a corpus-based approach to grammar such as Sinclair's. Is it any wonder he steers clear of such critics, choosing rather to insist doggedly on the sufficiency of his data rather than speculate on the 'infinite and productive nature' of language? This is a randomly chosen text-book, but it is recent, by a senior academic linguist, and shows clear awareness of corpora; similar views expressed a generation ago would probably not have used the term 'corpus' at all. Hence it is very probable that two decades worth of corpus linguistics has made little impression on the generativists' encampment and that the gulf between extreme versions of two radically opposed views remains as wide as ever. It does not of course follow that an interest in cognition and an interest in corpora are inherently irreconcilable.

Let us tiptoe cautiously into no-man's land by considering what I have characterised as a middle area of prediction failure, in which grammars are too coarse, or too 'idealised'. One aspect of this coarseness which corpora have exposed quite ruthlessly is that of restrictions. Take voice. Both traditional and recent generative descriptions usually see the passive as derived from the active or at least as a member of a set of complementary voice options (active, middle, passive). They usually cover routine problems thrown up by the transitivity system (e.g. verbs such as *cost*), but they fall short with highly transitive verbs like *take* because they are too unsophisticated to account for performance data. In particular, they are not good at predicting or explaining the non-occurrence of sentences such as: *No part should be taken by children under the age of ten.* In an exchange in *Applied*

Linguistics some years ago (Owen 1993; Francis & Sinclair 1994), I was reproved for suggesting, on the basis of introspection, that the sentence printed above is marginally more acceptable than the same sentence without the qualifier at the beginning, i.c. *Part should be taken by children under the age of ten.* My suggestion came in the context of an attempt to summarise Sinclair's view that the separation of grammar from lexis is artificial and untenable, in the course of which I noted that the susceptibility to 'passivization' (an unacceptable term to those who reject talk of derivation) of delexical expressions with *take* varied considerably. The broader point I was addressing was not at all original — Halliday had made it much more succinctly many years before — but it is that the theoretical limit of delicacy is the one-member class. As we shall see, that is also the theme which preoccupies Sinclair in his 1991 paper on *of.* This is how Halliday put the matter originally:

> No grammar has, it is believed, achieved the degree of delicacy required for the reduction of all such items (i.e. words — CO) to one-member classes, although provided the model can effectively handle cross-classification it is by no means absurd to set this as the eventual aim: that is a unique description for each item by its assignment to a 'microclass', which represents its value as the product of the intersection of a large number of classificatory dimensions.   (Halliday 1966:149)

In such a delicate grammar, *a look, part* and *account*, when part of a semi-fixed phrase such as *take a look, take part* or *take account of*, all have their 'own particular grammar', one aspect of which concerns premodification. Francis and Sinclair recorded a failure of intuition on my part concerning *No part should be taken*, since there was no evidence for this precise sequence ever occurring in the Bank of English. They were right about that at the time, and a quick search of today's Bank of English and Google (which appeared only in 1998) suggests they are still right. Or are they?

A failure of any grammatical statement to predict performance is ultimately not so interesting if it is confined to just one precise sequence of words. As the above-quoted extract from Carnie notes, there are limitless sequences which one might expect or hope to find in a corpus, but which are not there; so for a statement to fail interestingly, it must surely be in respect of grammatical potential. A grammatical prediction that passivized delexical expressions are slightly more acceptable (and thus more likely) if they are supplemented in some way (*A closer look..., No account..., No part...,* etc.) has wider scope than one particular expression. On the other hand, when the statement is accompanied by a note that this tendency varies, i.e. it applies more to some delexical expressions than to others, it clearly veers back towards a search for a more delicate lexically based explanation.

So what evidence is there for the predictive accuracy of my original intuition-based statement? Happily, the current Bank of English corpus confirms the essence quite well. There are approximately 100 lines representing the structure: (slot)+ *account* + (BE) + *taken*, and very frequently the slot is filled by a word such as *no* or *little*, e.g. *in calculating the Tax Index for 1997/8 no account has been taken of the impact of introducing Self-Assessment in the coming tax year.* There are also lines where the slot remains empty, as in: *Account should be taken of the considerable loss of earnings suffered by students while attending courses*, but fewer of these than the other type. Turning to *take a look*, we have the following lines supporting the statement very clearly:

```
In 1971, another look was taken at the Town Plan and again in 1978 and 1987.
    A proper look is being taken into why British consumers have to pay so much
Another look will also be taken at sponsorship to make it more appealing
If a cold hard look is not taken at the structure of the sport very soon
    a fresh look had to be taken at how such exercises were conducted in future
```

As I say, there is no corpus evidence for *No part should be taken*, but a Google trawl does yield: *No part taken in decision*, a headline from a report for the ethics commissioner of the province of Alberta. It looks to be extremely rare, and it is also telegraphic headline text. Nonetheless, rarity though it is, it occupies a distant point on a continuum of decomposability of delexical expressions, which in this matter of variation share properties with the wider class of 'fixed expressions' (cf. Moon 1998).

Like a lepidopterist, I have hunted down and caught my specimen, which is not even a very healthy one. I have done this only to show that it is not mandatory to treat grammatical statements derived from introspection as invalid merely on the grounds of sparse or non-existent corpus evidence. To some readers, and to Professor Carnie if he ever reads this, that will look like a statement of the obvious that I have taken an unconscionably long time to arrive at, especially since mainstream mentalist grammatical thinking holds it as an article of faith in any case. On the other hand, in the matter of representativeness, it really is remarkable that generative grammarians such as Carnie claim superiority, since even if corpora are never comprehensive, they are certainly very good at showing us what is typical — far better than any amount of introspection. To concede that is not the same thing as conceding that introspection is always misleading — far from it. It is actually quite amusing that the generativist's disdain for performance data is fully matched by the corpus linguist's disdain for introspection, and perhaps both parties would do well to remember that *representativeness* bears more than one shade of interpretation. Still, there is no doubt that it is in this area of typicality that Sinclair has scored most of his points and it serves as a useful departure point for our more detailed investigation of his classic paper on *of*.

3.   Summary of Sinclair's view of *of*

Some readers will be familiar with Sinclair's 'The Meeting of Lexis and Grammar' (1991:81–98), but for those who are not I present a précis of the main points before commenting separately. Henceforth, page number references to the article appear in the form (83), i.e. *Corpus, Concordance, Collocation*, p. 83.

We will pass over the opening section, which consists of a ritual denunciation of other grammarians' supposedly chaotic treatment of *of* (especially Quirk et al. 1985), and jump in at the point where Sinclair is at his combative best:

> It may ultimately be distracting to regard *of* as a preposition at all. I can think of no parallel classification in language or anywhere else. We are asked to believe that the word which is by far the commonest member of its class (more than double the next) is not normally used in the structure which is by far the commonest structure for the class. Doubts about whether *be* should be considered a verb or not are not as common as this. (83)

The data-observations underpinning this amazement and doubt are that the principal role of the preposition is to introduce a prepositional phrase in an adjunct, e.g. *She lives **in France***, whereas the principal role of *of* is as an element in a noun group (NG) (traditionally viewed as an embedded postmodifying PP), e.g. *the population **of France***. The central thrust of Sinclair's article then emerges in the following:

> It is not unreasonable to expect that quite a few of the very common words in the language are so unlike the others that they should be considered as unique, one-member word classes. If that status is granted to *of*, then there is no substantial difference between a dictionary entry for the word and a section of a grammar devoted to it. The one-member class is the place where grammar and lexis join. (83).

This leads to a discussion of the status of the headword in NGs consisting of N1 + *of* + N2. Examples such as *a couple of weeks* or *a bottle of Champagne* are problematic because they seem to refer to *weeks* and *Champagne* rather than *couples* and *bottles*. The headword is the only non-omissible element of an NG, and in many expressions containing *of* it is the noun following *of* which seems less omissible. "It is reasonable to expect the headword of a nominal group to be the principal reference point to the physical world," Sinclair argues (87). He therefore proposes a more general category of 'focus' N1 nouns, similar to the quantitive/partitive examples above, and deriving its coherence from the fact that it is N2 which is what the NG is really about; for example *the end of the day, the horns of the bull, the sound of his feet* principally refer to *day, bull* and *feet*, while *end, sound* and *horns* can be allocated to three slightly different sub-categories of 'focus'. *Horns*, for instance, are a 'specialized part' of the *bull* (an insight hard to rebut). A category of 'support' nouns follows, including many relatively semantically empty nouns such as *sort, kind* etc. and metaphorical examples such as *the treadmill of housework*.

Then we come to 'double-headed' NGs where: "neither noun seems to be pivotal or dominant, and where the structure simply requires both of them" (90). An important sub-class is 'nominalizations', i.e. "the type where there is something approximating to a propositional relationship between the two nouns" (91), such as the *enthusiastic collaboration of the auctioneers*, which could be paraphrased as *the auctioneers collaborate enthusiastically*. Anyone even slightly familiar with Sinclair's work will not be surprised to see how he hastens to pour cold water on any thought that paraphrases have real relevance to the grammar of such NGs: "It is…unnecessary to describe one structure as derived from another, and it is a complication which tends to ignore the function of *of*" (91). Double-headedness is also said to apply to cases which, but for modification of N1, might have been classified as instances of 'focus'. For example, in *a little shrill gasp of shock*, while the principal referent may still be *shock*, "It is clear that the secondary role of N1 is much enhanced by modification"(93). This is where our earlier example *the curious behaviour of the man* fits in. Because there are still examples unaccounted for by the foregoing, Sinclair 'mops up' with a not too bulging ragbag, but including a category of "relatively fixed phrases…of little structural interest" which looks suspiciously diverse and open-ended. The conclusion restates Sinclair's aim to persuade us of the fused nature of lexis and grammar. The paper is arguably as much a statement of methodological principles as it is about the particular word *of*, but since *of* is the subject matter, we too must inspect it closely.

4. Engaging with Sinclair's argument

Sinclair's first challenge concerns the classification of *of* as a preposition. Is it so very unusual? Consider *very*. This is the commonest member of the class adverb. The commonest function of adverbs is to add information about the predication element of the clause, as traditionally covered by the manner/place/time labels. True, adverbs also modify adjectives and other adverbs, and there are discourse adverbs, but the clause component role is the principal one. *Very* does not modify verbs **at all**, so it does not do what most adverbs do. At least some instances of *of* do look straightforwardly prepositional. Or consider noun modifiers such as materials. Dictionaries, including Cobuild's three editions (1987, 1995, 2001) treat *plaster* as in *plaster bust, ceiling, dinosaur* etc. as (N) and *plastic* as in *plastic bucket, window, dinosaur* etc. as (ADJ). Doubtless compilers have their reasons, perhaps subconsciously influenced by the morphology of *plastic*. Wherever one turns one finds this sort of issue, so the classification of *of* is perhaps just a severe instance of the complex interaction between form, function and distributional frequency in the allocation of words to classes. We might also ask why it is necessary for *of* to belong to only one class. The traditional classification as preposition could be retained for some uses, while we search for another label for other uses. In the case of *very*, it is quite normal to downplay its adverb class membership and stress its more precise function as submodifier or intensifier or some such. The issue here is not that *of* is not a very unusual word — it is — but rather whether it should be favoured with some uniquely special reward of being granted its own class; other prepositions, especially *for* and *to* are also very odd in their different ways. In Halliday's original conception, the principle of the one-member class can, or perhaps does, apply to any word and it is interesting that Sinclair implies a restriction on the principle. Doubtless in the end it is a matter of practicality and space in that going obsessively into the individual grammar of every word in the lexicon offers diminishing returns. Yet one feels reading this paper that Sinclair's arguments about *of* really serve as a vehicle for more far-reaching theoretical claims, which a consideration of other words, including some other prepositions, does not support.

The argument that *of* is not a preposition is two-pronged. According to Sinclair, not only does it not introduce PPs in adjuncts, but it also does not introduce PPs as NG postmodifiers. So, in *a bottle of champagne, the horns of the bull* or *a little shrill gasp of shock*, there are no postmodifying elements. The rightmost noun N2 is said either to be the head, or to share the status of head with N1. Sinclair is "not concerned with the niceties of syntax" (86) but we can indulge ourselves and consider for a moment how or whether constituent analysis of N1 + *of* might be done. For example, in *the horns of the bull*, if *bull* is H, how do we analyse *the horns of*? Granted, this question tends not to be asked about conventionalised measures such as *a lot of* or *a couple of*, which are treated as lexicalised quantifiers. We are able to treat them in this way by virtue of what Sinclair drolly dismisses as the "hallowed criterion of substitutability" (82); they are semantically and functionally equivalent to single word quantifiers such as *many* or *two*: *many/a lot of old professors, two/a couple of old professors* etc. Once we open the way for *the horns of, the udders of* and *the trunk of*, standard constituent structure analysis of the premodifying element of the NG cannot easily cope because no obvious slot is available. Sinclair's proposed new lexically-based categories seem to be some kind of open-ended widening of the quantifier/partitive slot: "the notion of quantifier or partitive can be extended into a general area of focus" (87). Open-ended? Not entirely.

The subsequent treatment of premodified N1 + N2 structures as double-headed is apparently forced on him by the inescapable need to separate those premodifiers as constituents. In *a little shrill gasp of shock*, the modifying adjectives *little* and *shrill* have to modify something, i.e. a head noun. They clearly do not modify *shock* so we are left with no alternative but to treat *gasp* as a head — one of two. Sinclair says: "Neither N1 nor N2 can easily be omitted because N1 is treated as a full headword" (93). The appearance of *full* in this sentence is perplexing. It suggests a contrast with other headwords which are 'partial'. But that runs counter to the argument, which is that N1 in categories such as 'focus' is not H — not partial H, simply not H at all. In any case, how can there be degrees of H-ness?

In fact, I think there is a way we can allow degrees of H-ness, but accepting this may have irksome implications for grammarians who profess not to be interested in cognition, or who subscribe to a model of production involving some sort of sharp switching between an 'idiom principle' and an 'open-choice principle'. Let us concede that mechanical application of constituent structure analysis in which *of* is an undisputed preposition might lead to counter-intuitive results. Essentially that is why quantifiers such as *a couple of* are conventionally treated as such. It is also my experience that undergraduates often assign headedness to N2 in constructions of the kind we have been discussing on the grounds that N2 is what the NG is 'about'. Interestingly, they also do this with other prepositions. It may be

Head?	Expression	Comment	OT
N2	A lot of money	quantifier	fail
N1??+N2	A load of money	measure	fail
N1?+N2	A bag of money	less conventional measure	fail
N1?+N2	A history of money	e.g. of JMS 'focus'? "component, aspect or attribute"	fail
N1+N2	A hatred of money	propositional: x hates money (less fixed expression?)	fail
N1+N2	A waste of money	propositional: x wastes money (fixed expression?)	what a waste!
N1?+N2?	A bait of money	a. money laid as a bait b. bait consisting of money	a. fail b. pass
N1+N2?	A reward of money	*of*-phrase seems to add secondary info., qualifying H	pass
N1+N2???	A photograph of money	ditto, even more so.	pass
N1	A child of money	*of*-phrase clearly qualifying H	pass

Figure 1. Gradience analysis of headedness of N1 + *of* + N2 nominal groups

useful to attack the problem by means of gradience analysis. Figure 1 is designed to show that you can move by small increments from a feeling that N2 is a unique head, through various stages to a feeling that N1 is a unique head. Question-marks are a code for calibrating the possibility that N1 or N2 'shares headedness' with its partner N. OT stands for 'omissibility test', i.e. do you damage the meaning of the whole expression if you omit *of* + N2? Omissibility is surely determined to a greater extent by the discourse context than Sinclair acknowledges — thieves sharing loot might well say: *gimme a bag*, and they don't mean crisps — but we can allow that as contingent; he would certainly be aware of it.

Readers may react variously to these examples and comments, but whatever individual thoughts one has, it should not be too hard to agree that one's sense of the information weighting shifts from N2 to N1 as one goes down the examples. The first example is about money, a lot of it; the last is about a child, a certain kind of child. Other prepositions share these characteristics. As Sinclair reminds us, their usual role is to introduce adjuncts, but suppose we find that our sense of information weighting in NGs, as determined by an omissibility test, leads us to think of N2 as H. What are the implications?

Prep.	Context	OT
for	Evidence gathered by the French counter-espio-nage agency, La Direction de la Surveillance du Territoire (DST), points to **plans for a series of atrocities in France**, the court in Paris will be told	?points to plans ✓points to a series of atrocities in France
on	On **women's increasing focus on domestic duties in prosperous households**, see Cott, *Bonds of Womanhood*, 43–45	?women's increasing focus ✓women's increasing domestic duties
to	Ireland's home games will be exclusively live on our channels," he said. We have also exclusively secured **the rights to the finals in South Korea and Japan in 2002**.	?secured the rights (in 2002) ✓secured the finals in S.Korea and Japan in 2002
with	It's one thing, Civic Liberals could argue, for the rich to be able to buy the nicest cars, or **the houses with the nicest views**. It's another thing to make it easy for money to buy life itself.	?(buy)…the houses ✓(buy)…the nicest views

Figure 2. Omissibility of 'postmodifying' PPs with *for, on, to* and *with*.

In the first example, perhaps we should say that *series* is H, not *plans*. Or on second thoughts, perhaps it is *atrocities* — that seems to be what this is really about. We would then have recursion within Sinclair's 'focus' category to deal with: *plans for a series of*. Of course, the reason the omissibility test fails is because of the vagueness of *plans* and the quantitative nature of *series*.

Let us recall *the curious behaviour of the man* and *the curious incident of the dog in the night-time*. Although Quirk et al. receive little credit, the following remark seems to me to be rather helpful:

> According to the principle of end-focus, the genitive tends to give information focus to the head noun, whereas the *of*-construction tends to give focus to the prepositional complement...this principle is congruent with the preference for the *of*-construction with partitive and appositive meaning, where the genitive would result in undesirable or absurd final prominence: *the problem's part, *his resignation's shock   (Quirk et al. 1985:323)

Thus, genitive: *the bull's horns* — focus on *horns*; *of*-construction: *the horns of the bull* — focus on *bull*. Similarly: the *part of the problem* — focus on *problem*. Now it may just be a curious co-incidence of terms, but is there not a striking connection between Quirk's comment on 'end-focus' and Sinclair's proposed category of 'focus' nouns, i.e. nouns which precede an 'end-focussed' noun? The difference between their positions is that Quirk remains content to distinguish focus (an information-weighting issue) from headedness (a structural issue), whereas Sinclair wants to fuse them. *The dog in the night-time's curious incident* would, in Quirk's terms, give *incident* undesirable or absurd prominence. Yes it would, but why? Quirk's only clue in the above citation is the word 'appositive', which defines the relationship between the two Ns. In *the shock of his resignation*, *the shock* **is** the *resignation*, just as *the incident* **is** *the dog in the night-time*. Grammarians interested in language awareness will say speakers know about these relationships and can provide suitable paraphrases for them, just as I have. The sixty paragraphs for *of* in the OED are a magnificent if messy attempt to cover the range of relationships. Generative grammarians see sentences lurking within these structures — layers of sentences, even; but not just generative grammarians. For while Sinclair characteristically huffs his disapproval: "finding equivalent clauses for examples seems to offer a misleading interpretation of the nominal group, as compared with the 'focus' classification which relies on collocation and the conventional associations we make in the light of our experience of the world" (92), that does not stop him from using the term 'nominalization' as his major sub-category of double-headed examples; nominalization of what?

There are interesting parallels between the NGs we have been looking at here and the delexical expressions we looked at earlier (e.g. *take a look, take part* etc.) In Sinclair's model, selection of any of these examples is made according to the 'idiom principle', i.e. as a single lexical choice. In both cases, the information weighting of a constituent is shifted rightwards. Although he has not to my knowledge commented specifically on the 'headedness' of delexical structures, we can safely assume that he would reject any analysis which treats *take* as the head of a predicate structure. Thus, in delexical structures the shift is from verb to noun (*take* to *look*), and in 'focus' structures from N1 to N2 (*horns* to *bull*). As Sinclair himself puts it, "some 'meanings' of very frequent words seem to have very little meaning at all, for example, *take*, in *take a look at this...*" (112). At first sight, the comparison creaks a little when one begins to consider whether the N1s in 'focus' groups are also lexically diminished since in *the horns of the bull*, the horns are surely meaningful enough. It makes more sense though if one pays as much attention to 'grammaticalization' as to 'delexicalization', the two processes being in an inverse relationship. The corollary of *take* losing 'nearly all meaning' is that it becomes 'nearly all grammatical' — a feature we recognise as general and defining for 'grammatical' words. When Sinclair says that N1 has a 'focus' relationship to N2, he is trying to capture the process of 'grammaticalization' which has begun to creep over N1, a process which is accessible to intuition, as evidenced in decisions of novice grammarians such as undergraduates.

The process of grammaticalization can be put into reverse. For example, we saw earlier that delexical verbs can be passive if the noun is modified, as in *If a cold hard look is not taken at the structure of the sport very soon*. The supposedly fixed idiom has been subjected to decomposition. Modification emphasises the 'nouniness' of *look*, which was tinged with 'verbiness' in the normal version. For Sinclair this decomposition perhaps represents a switch to the 'open-choice' principle; open choice of what exactly? The passive version of an expression which is normally active, I propose. Similarly, when Sinclair says that modification of *gasp* in *a little shrill gasp of shock*, makes *gasp* a 'full' head noun, resulting in 'double-headedness', this is a movement back leftwards of the information-weighting. The grammaticalization of *gasp* has been somewhat reversed.

In the end, Sinclair's labels of 'focus', 'support', 'double-headed' and so forth do describe real facts about information-weighting. Using the power of the concordancer, they certainly do this more comprehensively than other descriptions and they concentrate our minds on the difficult task of producing a model which is both general enough to be structurally robust yet sensitive enough to accommodate our sense of these information-weighting issues: I repeat — our sense of these information-weighting issues — our awareness in other words. There are surely many points in our grammatical models where the rigidities of conventional structure analysis conflict with our sense of the information a message is conveying. Martin (1993:238), following Halliday on grammatical metaphor, refers to the problem as one of degrees of 'congruence'. The problem starts as soon as one makes first steps in grammar. *One man was repeatedly caught on a bull's horns* says a newspaper report. Many novice grammarians find it hard to accept that *One man* is subject, — 'Surely *one man* is the object? It's the bull that's doing the catching! Or the horns anyway...' they protest. We know better and teach the importance of keeping structure and semantics apart, at least until you are equipped to bring them together again, whether by invoking deep structure or some other explanatory model such as Sinclair's. In this sense, Sinclair's paper on *of* is in good company because it tackles a problem which other grammars are also deeply concerned with.

5.   Conclusion — Sinclair's niche in the Pantheon

Sinclair's contribution to the study of grammar is probably the most contentious aspect of his multi-faceted achievement. There are certainly more famous grammarians but I suggest that he more than any other 20th century linguist has attempted to shift our view of what grammar actually is. That claim may strike some readers as hyperbole. What about Chomsky? While it can hardly be disputed that Chomsky heads the fame league, it is also possible to see his mentalist rationalism as a less radical departure from grammatical tradition than Sinclair's unrelenting empiricism.

Teubert (2004:78 ff.) has argued somewhat differently. By focussing our attention on cognition, he says, Chomsky has changed 'the agenda' for linguistics, whereas Sinclair's corpus linguistics represents a return to a pre-modern hermeneutic tradition, in which linguistic description (categories, paradigms, rules etc.) had an exegetical function, typically for classical texts in 'dead' languages, but was not at all concerned with 'productivity'. This is an interesting, and in some ways unexpected, position. It is usual to associate radical shifts in agenda with progress — the Kuhnian thesis in other words — and the literature abounds with phrases like 'the Chomskyan revolution' to describe what people believe to be significant progress in linguistics. Even the severest critics of Chomsky (e.g. Sampson 2005) tend to engage with him on his chosen agenda-changing territory, i.e. cognition and the mind. Teubert seems to doubt the value of trying to change the agenda — not only in this instance but perhaps in principle. Instead, it is Sinclair's rootedness in a text-analytic tradition which embodies the true purpose of linguistics and thus of grammar. What many linguists, and not just Chomskyans, would regard as atavism, Teubert interestingly elevates into a virtue. In other words, Sinclair may not be radical, but he is right.

What one means by tradition is a matter of historical perspective. When Mao was asked how the French revolution had affected the course of history, he is famously said to have replied: "It is too early to tell." Teubert's exact scope for 'premodern' is left a little unclear, but he briefly traces the move away from traditional hermeneutics as beginning with the evolution of nineteenth century comparative philology and developing into twentieth century structuralism. So even in Teubert's account it is quite possible to understand Chomskyan linguistics as the culmination of a rather protracted process of paradigm shift. About 150 years elapsed between Humboldt's (1963/1827–1829) point about language making "infinite use of finite means" and Chomsky's well-known and repeated reference to it (e.g. 1965:8). Chomsky himself of course identifies his thought with a much older rationalist tradition stretching back at least as far as classical hermeneutics. Perhaps we should expect any defence of theory to seek to counterbalance claims of innovation with an appeal to historical roots, and perhaps we should treat such appeals with a certain scepticism. The challenge represented by corpus linguistics has arisen in less than 20 years and even its boldest adherents might admit that it is a bit early to tell whether it truly represents a more radical break with the past than generative linguistics, or whether it in fact continues a much older historical tradition.

In short, we cannot address questions of shifts in perspective in terms of time alone. The view that pre-modern linguists were unconcerned with productivity is amplified by Teubert as follows: "Their aim was not to produce new texts in these languages; they wanted to understand the texts we had inherited from ancient times. The rules they came up with were rules to help us make sense of the sentences. The rules were meant to describe what we were confronted with in the texts; they were not designed to empower us to become competent speakers of ancient Greek" (Teubert 2004:78). This implies that 'productivity' is a characteristic of language users rather than of language; that it is the same as the individual's capacity to become proficient. 'Productivity' could be used to mean this, but more typically in the literature, following Hockett (1960:90), it refers to an abstract property of language itself, enabling both production and comprehension of novel utterances. That is how Carnie uses it in my earlier citation. This property exists independently of whether novel utterances are in fact produced and also of the capacity of the individual competently to produce any. In this more usual sense, ancient or 'dead' languages like Greek, Hebrew and Latin exhibit productivity no less than living languages. Pre-modern linguists were perfectly well aware of this. So in stating the rules for the 'ablative absolute' or the 'accusative and infinitive', the Latin grammarian was not merely saying 'this is a means for you to understand certain revered texts by Tacitus' but also 'this is a generalisation about Latin — this is how Latin works.'

So while pre-modern linguistics was doubtless motivated by a hermeneutic imperative, it necessarily engaged with productivity because, as far as I can see, all linguistics does. The claim that Chomsky represents a 'turn', or even the endpoint of a 150-year turn, in respect of a focus on productivity seems not at all as clear as it might be. What is clear is that computers with the power to store, sort and make available vast amounts of data in an instant have been around for only a short time. Sinclair's use of this technology may be a catalyst for a renewal of energy in hermeneutics, but it is open to question whether Sinclair himself regards that as a primary aim. Rather, it seems to me that his aim has been to challenge very long-held assumptions about grammar. As suggested above, grammatical tradition would regard the relationship between active and passive, or between *of* + NG and genitive constructions or between certain instances of *of* + NG and a proposition as manifestations of productivity, commonly referred to as rules, and in more cognitive accounts as generative. While Sinclair tends to wave such notions aside as 'unnecessary' or 'distracting', his position is not really sustainable. In his grammar for learners of English (1990), he briefly discusses 'productive features':

> ...we set out many 'productive features' to guide the student towards confidence in personal expression...by describing the language in this way, we give plenty of scope for creativity and innovation, a feature which is not commonly found in grammars. There are many productive features in current English...A productive feature invites and encourages us to use our imagination. The list of words and phrases that will fit a structure is often impossible to define completely. There may be a number of words in regular use, but in addition to that many other possibilities, offering the user a safe place to experiment.   (Sinclair 1990:ix–x)

These are most interesting remarks, since they promise that learners will, following the advice of this book, say all sorts of innovative, creative, yet grammatical, things, and that there is in principle no limit to these. Carnie could not have put it better, except that he would probably cavil at the idea of there being 'many' productive features — how many? And is some of the language produced without using them?

The reason for arguing that Sinclair is the most radical 20th century grammarian is his challenge to cognitive models and his unbending insistence on deriving grammatical statements from recorded usage, i.e. a corpus. It has had a massive influence. No grammar today, not even generative grammar (as we saw in the citation from Carnie) pretends that corpora do not tell us anything interesting. Yet the ostensible chief objection to cognitive models, which is that evidence from introspection is too unreliable, is debatable in terms of both the extent of that unreliability and its true theoretical significance. The belief that grammar is something one must do with as little introspection as possible, that the task of the grammarian is simply to describe performance data and not to speculate on what speakers know, is in fact belied by the fascinating data which Sinclair serves up for us. Clearly there is an uncomfortable gap between the coarse classification of *of* as a preposition and the more subtle, in context constantly adjusting, balance between the lexical and grammatical functions of this, and indeed every, word. But speakers do have feelings about this. They are alive to the gradience of information-weighting in NGs with *of*. Terms such as 'nominalization', 'delexicalization' and my 'grammaticalization' point to psychological processes. If we wanted to, we could also explore this diachronically — *of* has previous, to put it mildly.

So Sinclair is truly radical, but he is also — dare I say it? — caught on the horns of a dilemma. The left horn is tradition — and its conspicuous failure to match performance data. This one he has largely blunted and disabled. The right horn is knowledge and its relation to productivity. This one he has never properly grasped, let alone blunted, and it is still sticking into him.

When John read my paper on *of* he wrote to me. I had expected him to be annoyed. Instead, to my relief, he was interested and observant, asking several detailed questions, and hinting at plans he had for further work on lexis and grammar. Clearly his mind was as alert and fertile as ever, and his letter was a final reminder to me of how he always saw beyond what the rest of us see. That is a rare gift and I am sure I speak for many when I say that I continue to feel his influence in my daily thoughts about language.

References

Carnie, A. (2002). *Syntax: A Generative Introduction*. Oxford: Blackwell.

Chomsky N. (1965). *Aspects of the Theory of Syntax*. Cambridge, Mass: The M.I.T. Press.

Collins Cobuild English Language Dictionary. (1987). London/Glasgow: Collins. Second edition published as *Collins Cobuild English Dictionary* (1995), London/Glasgow: HarperCollins. Third edition published as *Collins Cobuild English Dictionary for Advanced Learners* (2001), London/Glasgow: HarperCollins.

Francis, G. &. Sinclair, J. M. (1994). 'I bet he drinks Carling Black Label': a riposte to Owen on corpus grammar. *Applied Linguistics*, 15 (2), 190–200.

Halliday, M. A. K. (1970). *A Course in Spoken English: Intonation*. Oxford: Oxford University Press.

Halliday, M. A. K. (1966). Lexis as a linguistic level. In C. E. Bazell et al. (Eds.), *In Memory of J.R. Firth*. London: Longman.

Hockett, C. F. (1960). The origin of speech. *Scientific American*, 203, 88–96

Humboldt, W. von (1963/1827–1829). *Schriften zur Sprachphilosophie — Ueber die Verschiedenheiten des menschlichen Sprachbaues*. In Humboldt's *Werke*, vol. III. Darmstadt: Wissenschaftliche Buchgesellschaft.

Mackin, R. (1967). *A Course in Spoken English: Texts, Drills and Tests*. London: Oxford University Press

Martin, J. R. (1993). Life as a noun: arresting the universe in science and humanities. In M. A. K. Halliday & J. R. Martin (Eds.), *Writing Science* (pp. 221–67). Pittsburgh: University of Pittsburgh Press.

Moon, R. E. (1998). *Fixed Expressions and Idioms in English: A Corpus-based Approach*. Oxford: Oxford University Press.

Owen, C. R. (1993). Corpus-based grammar and the Heineken effect: lexico-grammatical description for language learners. *Applied Linguistics*, 14 (2), 167–187.

Quirk, R., Greenbaum, S., Leech, G., & Svartvik, J. (1985). *A Comprehensive Grammar of The English Language*. London: Longman.

Sampson, G. (2005). *The 'Language Instinct' Debate*. London: Continuum. (Revised Edition of Sampson, G. (1997), *Educating Eve*.)

Sinclair, J. M. (1991). *Corpus, Concordance, Collocation*. Oxford: Oxford University Press. (Chapter 6, 'The meeting of lexis and grammar', was first published in 1989 in M. L. Tickoo (Ed.) *Learners' Dictionaries: State of the Art*, SEAMEO Regional Language Centre, Singapore.)

Sinclair, J. M. (1990). (Ed.) *Collins COBUILD English Grammar*. London: Collins.

Sinclair, J. M. (1972). *A Course in Spoken English: Grammar*. Oxford: Oxford University Press.

Teubert, W. (2004). Language and corpus linguistics. In M. A. K. Halliday, W. Teubert, C. Yallop & A. Čermáková, *Lexicology and Corpus Linguistics* (pp. 73–112). London: Continuum.

Sinclair, pattern grammar and the question of *hatred*

Wolfgang Teubert
University of Birmingham

The view of pattern grammar is that syntactic structures and lexical items are co-selected and that grammatical categories begin to align very closely with semantic distinctions. While this is certainly a valid position when analysing the phenomenon of collocation, it does not really solve the problem for open choice issues. Not all language use can be subsumed under the idiom principle. The noun *hatred*, for instance, can co-occur with any discourse object for which hatred can be expressed. It can also co-occur with other lexical items standing for various circumstantial aspects. The grammatical structure itself often does not tell us whether we find expressed the object of hatred or some circumstantial aspect, as these structures tend to have more than one reading. Lexicogrammar, or local grammar, is more than equating a syntactic structure with a semantic pattern. We have to be aware of the different functions or readings a given grammatical structure can have. The framework of valency/dependency grammar can help us to make the necessary distinctions.

Keywords: grammar, pattern grammar, valency, phraseology, meaning

1. Introduction

I learned corpus linguistics from John Sinclair, and therefore it is not surprising that I share his vision of most aspects of this field. That this does not so much apply to grammar may result from the fact that I spent the first third of my career investigating German grammar. This has, no doubt, biased my view.

German belongs to the more traditional of the Indo-European languages with a strongly developed morphology, an elaborate system of inflections, but a comparatively liberal word order. The humanists tried, not always successfully, to model it on Latin, and the standardisation efforts of the 19th century that accompanied the trend towards compulsory primary school were inspired by the early philologists.

They made sure that no conjugation and declension pattern was lost, rare and expendable as it might be.

The German grammar I was taught at university was largely still formulated in the Neo-Grammarian paradigm. The parts of speech, the constituents of the sentence, the description of phrases and clauses were still widely informed by Latin grammar. Obvious deficiencies of the model led to a reformulation in the sixties of the last century. In the area I am concerned with in this paper, namely nouns and their modifiers, this was the advent of valency grammar. Today, we find different versions of it. The framework in which I discuss valency grammar in this paper is laid out in Ulrich Engel's *Syntax der deutschen Gegenwartssprache* (1977). Valency is the property of virtually all verbs, many nouns, some adjectives (mostly in predicative use) and a few adverbs to admit certain syntactically defined phrases while excluding certain other syntactically defined phrases. Thus, some verbs allow direct objects but not indirect objects, some allow only indirect objects, and some allow both. Valency grammar goes together with dependency theory. Objects are described as depending on the (main) verb of a sentence or a clause. We can observe similar conditions for nouns, particularly nouns derived from verbs. Here the modifiers of the head noun, called 'Attribute' in the German tradition, depend on the head noun, which, in turn, depends on the (main) verb. The modifiers I am interested in in this paper are possessives and prepositional phrases. Valency here is the faculty of (valent) nouns to admit, as complements, certain kinds of prepositional phrases while excluding phrases with other prepositions. I can say *their hatred towards the enemy* but not *their hatred at the enemy*. The prepositional phrase depends on the noun *hatred*; and it is its valency that accounts for what is possible and what is not.

Originally, valency was thought of as a model of a solely syntactic description. For verbs, this might work, up to a point. The relationship between a verb and an indirect object does not need necessarily to be defined in semantic terms. But for nouns, the case looks different. A phrase such as *the hatred of a million coolies* is, in semantic terms, inherently ambiguous, both readings residing in one syntactic form. Is it the coolies who hate or is it the coolies who are hated? This leads to a dissociation between syntactic form and semantic value, the concern with the latter being inspired by Charles Fillmore's seminal paper 'The case for case' (1968). It was on this basis that many years ago I investigated the valency of German nouns (Teubert 1979).

English is different. In many structural ways, it has moved away from the Indo-European family of languages. Morphology and inflection are almost gone. Instead, we now have a quite rigorous word order. As there are no morphological rules for compounding, it is better to talk about multi-word units. Once there are hardly any morphological and syntactic specifics to be observed, the meaning and discursive function of a given phrase becomes foregrounded while its syntactic structure seems to recede. This is why English asks for a different kind of grammar, a grammar as we find it in M. A. K. Halliday's systemic functional grammar. This is a paradigm that liberates our analyses of English sentences from the Procrustean coercions of a Continental style grammar as that of Randolph Quirk, Sidney Greenbaum, Geoffrey Leech and Jan Svartvik (Quirk et al. 1972). Pattern grammar went even further. Combining a Hallidayan approach with Sinclair's observations on grammar, it made a point of neglecting the relevance of the venerable categories of the Neo-Grammarians. But can patterns really replace syntax? Are we not throwing out the baby of meaning with the bathwater of syntactic distinctions? This is the lead question of this paper.

Valency is the Continental way to link local, lexical grammar to general grammar. Sinclair was among the first to insist that grammar and lexis cannot be separated: "One who asserts that lexical patterning is distinct from grammatical does so despite the knowledge that each word in a text has a grammatical function" (in Krishnamurthy 2004:3). Does lexical grammar do away with syntax, does it entail the promise that we do not need categories such as objects or complements, at least for a language like English? This seems to be the claim that some of Sinclair's collaborators make for pattern grammar. I am not convinced. Therefore I will have a deeper look at some of the modifiers of the noun *hatred* (and, where necessary, of some comparable nouns). I will argue that we need syntactic categories and classifications in order to do our job. Even if we discard some of the old ones, we have to replace them by categories defined in such a way that they can do their job better. Categories and classifications are, after all, not features of language as such only waiting to be discovered. They are linguistic inventions (and conventions), and it is the community of linguists who have to negotiate their applicability and usefulness. Valency grammar uses the framework of another Continental concoction, dependency grammar. In this paper, I will draw on both notions.

Sinclair is too much a theoretical thinker to reject the necessity of categories. He explicitly stated back in 1970: "Grammatical influence on the collocation is very strong; it frequently overshadows and cuts across lexical patterns of behaviour" (in Krishnamurthy 2004:16). How, then, do we have to imagine the relationship between grammar and semantic patterning? His answer to this question in 2004 is: "From a theoretical point of view, pattern grammars were designed to demonstrate that as you develop lexicogrammar in detail grammatical categories begin to align very closely with semantic distinctions" (in Krishnamurthy 2004:xxvii). I fully agree. But does pattern grammar give us the categories we need to make the distinctions? Can it distinguish between the two readings of *the hatred of a million coolies*? This is where I have some doubts.

We could argue, however, that for the reader the semantic ambiguity is hardly a problem. It is resolved in the wider context into which the phrase is embedded. The full sentence reads:

> All power, all profits, all our sources of livelihood are in their hands — but the one thing they leave behind will destroy them — the **hatred** *of a million coolies!* (BNC)

So it is the coolies who hate their colonisers. In this sentence, however, the *of*-phrase refers to the object of *hatred*:

> And if you look at what religions, organized religions exhibit, you will find, that organized religions are based on <u>fear and **hatred**</u> *of other people.* (BNC)

This is not due to the fact that *hatred* here is a part of a binomial, as this example shows:

> It is not the perspective of a man who is dominated by the <u>fear and **hatred**</u> *of Hellenizers.* (BNC)

Here it is the Hellenizers whose hatred he has to fear. Could it be the definite article that makes the difference? Apparently not:

> As far as I am concerned the desire to win, <u>the fear and **hatred**</u> *of losing,* is increased immensely by the knowledge that I have the maple leaf on my jersey. (BNC)

It seems to be fairly obvious, then, that *hatred* followed by an *of*-phrase has, out of context, two readings, and that these two readings must be correlated to two different syntactic descriptions.

Sinclair has devoted a chapter of his book *Corpus, Concordance, Collocation* (1991) to adnominal *of*-phrases. This chapter, 'The meeting of lexis and grammar', will be my starting point. I am deeply indebted to Charles Owen for his discussion of this chapter (see preceding paper). Even though he has a different focus, his paper has been a source of inspiration. Sinclair's views on the question whether many head nouns we encounter in connection with *of*-phrases should be rather taken as nodes of extended determiners or quantifiers is something I fully agree with. But this is not my concern here. I am looking at head nouns whose headedness is undisputed. These nouns and their patterns are described in the comprehensive pattern grammar compiled and authored by Sinclair's collaborators Gill Francis, Susan Hunston and Elizabeth Manning (Francis, Hunston & Manning 1998). There can be no doubt that Sinclair is sympathetic to their programme; his endorsement of pattern grammar, quoted above, is ample evidence. Grammatical categories, however, have to be posited on more than just the one level that we find in Francis, Hunston and Manning (1998). My goal is to propose a set of categories and classifications taken from valency theory that would augment pattern grammar in this respect. The infelicitous consequence is that the grammar/lexis relationship appears to be more complex than pattern grammar, as we know it now, would make us believe. But first we must have a closer look at Sinclair's suggestions for dealing with the adnominal *of*-phrase, and at their implementation in the Francis, Hunston and Manning grammar.

For corpus linguists, there is no evidence other than corpus evidence. For reasons of simplicity of access I have chosen to use the British National Corpus (BNC) as the source of my evidence; it is installed on my computer so that I can work offline.

2. The *of*-phrase according to John Sinclair

Sinclair focuses on *of*-phrases that modify nouns (Sinclair 1991:81–98). He discusses, at some length, the question whether we really should group *of*, which is so much more frequent than other prepositions, in the word class containing, for example, *against, among, besides, between, towards, at, in, on* etc. Indeed, there is a difference. What used to be the genitive in traditional Indo-European languages — i.e. an inflection form, a case most closely associated with nouns — has, over the last millennium, metamorphosed into a word, *of* in English, *de* in French, and similarly in other languages, into a word that is traditionally classified as a preposition. While many prepositions can be said to have (a sort of) meaning, *of* can be better described as taking over the functions the genitive had.

These are the groupings of the head nouns suggested by Sinclair (ibid.):

Conventional measures (genitivus partitivus): *both of them*
Less conventional measures (genitivus partitivus): *the bottle of port*
Focus on a part (genitivus possessivus): *the undersides of plates*
Focus on a specialised part (genitivus possessivus): *generations of men*
Support (genitivus explicativus): *the notion of machine intelligence*
Support (genitivus subiectivus): *the position of France*
Metaphor (genitivus explicativus): *the treadmill of housework*
Titles (not a genitive at all): *the Duchess of Bedford*
Nominalizations (genitivus obiectivus): *a wonderful sketch of her*
Nominalizations (genitivus subiectivus): *the growth of a single-celled creature*

There are eight categories according to Sinclair's proposal. In round brackets, I have added the equivalent that we would find in the Continental grammar tradition, informed by the Latin grammar. In the case of 'support' and 'nominalization' I have cited more than one of his examples whenever they would be assigned to different traditional categories. What does each of these groups have in common, and how do the examples given differ?

At this point I should draw the attention to the difference of goals which Sinclair has in his chapter and I have in this paper. Sinclair sets out to question the headedness of the first noun in a phrase such as *the position of France*. He maintains that this noun "is seen as offering some kind of support to N2", and he adds that "there are several ways in which this is done". He also refers to the Collins Cobuild English Grammar which lists these nouns as "nouns which are rarely used alone" (Sinclair 1990:89). The question of headedness is discussed in depth in Charles Owen's paper (this volume), and I will not comment on it here. My question is whether the old categories do not deliver what Sinclair is interested in while providing additional distinctions which might be useful, for instance to the language learner.

The first example of a support group noun is notion, in *the notion of machine intelligence*. Traditionally it would count as a genitivus explicativus (gen.expl.), and similarly with *the city of York*. The sentence *We discussed the notion of machine intelligence* is equivalent with the sentence *We discussed machine intelligence, which is a notion*. We find this *of*-group as modifier of nouns denoting concepts of abstract categories (*entirety, class, set, field, area, type* etc.), semi-abstract groupings such as *vice, virtue, property, fact, problem, risk* etc., geographical entities (*region, county, city* etc.), institutions (*university, church, council*), and content categories (*notion, theory, idea, invention* etc.). It is the same kind of genitive that we find in certain metaphors (like Sinclair's example *the treadmill of housework*). All these nouns are what Hunston and Francis call shell nouns (Hunston & Francis 1999:185), a very accurate description.

The other example, *the position of France*, however, is different. While *machine intelligence* __is__ *a notion, France* __has__ *a position*. France is an agent; it has and holds a position (in the words of the entry in the Cobuild dictionary: 'Your position on a particular matter is your attitude towards it or opinion of it'). This is not a gen. expl., this is a genitivus subiectivus (gen.subi.). Thus we can talk about *France's position on this issue*, but not about *machine intelligence's notion on this issue*. A gen.expl. never comes in the form of a prenominal possessive. Specimens of the gen.subi., however, frequently do. These are things a learner of English might find useful to know.

Nominalizations are nouns derived from verbs. They often inherit from them the faculty to express relationships with certain specified entities. In the case of verbs we call them subject and object(s), in the case of nouns they are usually called adnominal modifiers. In the case of nominalization, the subject of a verb often becomes a possessive (poss.) (i.e. a possessive pronoun or a Saxon genitive), or it becomes an *of*-phrase. The traditional Continental category is the gen.subi. already mentioned above. The equivalent of the direct object is often, though by no means always, also an *of*-phrase, although not a gen.subi., but, of course, a genitivus obiectivus (gen.obi.). Sinclair brings an example of each: *a wonderful sketch of her* (gen.obi.), and: *the growth of a single-celled creature* (gen.subi.). Sinclair is aware of the parallelism between the verbal and the nominal structure: "Certainly, it is easy to find equivalent clauses for these examples (['an arrangement of familiar figures' and] 'X arranges familiar figures', etc.). However, such an operation seems to offer a misleading interpretation of the nominal group, as compared with … the conventional associations we make in the light of our experience of the world" (Sinclair 1991: 92). Why would such an interpretation be misleading? We will come back to this issue, and I will try to show that the opposition between gen. subi. and gen.obi., in analogy to the categories of subject and object on the verb level, can be a useful distinction.

In this chapter of *Corpus, Concordance, Collocation,* Sinclair is more interested in the question of the 'headedness' of what is traditionally considered to be the head noun than in the issue of categories and classifications. He does not dismiss traditional views out of hand. When he revisits *of*-phrases, in his review of *The Longman Grammar of Spoken and Written English* (Sinclair 2001), he states very clearly: "It would not surprise me very much if the bulk of the vocabulary of English fell into the neat categories of class and structure that have been reserved for them for centuries" (Sinclair 2001:348), and he warns: "For if using a corpus to elucidate the grammar of a language does not lead to important advances and new insights, then the traditional way is probably the easier one" (Sinclair 2001:341). This admonition should also refer to the unwarranted renunciation of upper-level grammatical categories.

3. *Hatred* in the pattern grammar

The most comprehensive account of the concept and the theoretical aspects of pattern grammar can be found in Hunston and Francis' (1999) *Pattern Grammar.* The description of the patterns of head nouns modified by prepositional phrases and possessives is found in Francis, Hunston and Manning (1998) *Grammar Patterns 2: Nouns and Adjectives.* I will base my comments on some theoretical issues and on the treatment of the noun *hatred*.

Pattern grammar is about the association of grammatical structure with meaning. As Francis puts it (1993:142–3):

> It is an approach which recognises the importance of syntagmatic patterning and dependent lexical choices in the structuring of language. In other words, we take the view that syntactic structures and lexical items … are co-selected, and that it is impossible to look at one independently of the other… The interdependence of syntax and lexis is such that they are ultimately inseparable, and it becomes merely a methodological convenience to regard them as different perspectives from which to view language use.

Repeatedly Hunston and Francis (1999) quote Sinclair to this effect, for instance on page 83: "It seems that there is a strong tendency for sense and syntax to be associated". I read this as a reminder that we should view their pattern grammar as the implementation of Sinclair's programme.

What astonishes me, though, is how Hunston and Francis in this very context are eager to dispense with all grammatical categories other than parts of speech. This, they say, had not been their original intention. Rather, they had, at first, aimed "to have an explicit and consistent policy for each decision regarding [the traditional structural] categories used, so that the system of analysis would be both internally consistent and defendable". They would "reflect the traditional consensus of grammarians … regarding the categories of Object, Complement and so on." But then they "became increasingly disenchanted" with this task, "not merely because it turned out to be difficult to the point of impossibility, but because it seemed more and more futile." Hunston and Francis point out "that our rejection of structural analysis is not the result of a lack of thought or commitment" (Hunston & Francis 1999:151f.). Is it futile because the traditional grammatical categories do not work or because we do not need them? To me it seems that for Hunston and Francis the syntactic surface structure maps so one-to-one on to the meaning of the phrase that structure and meaning become almost indistinguishable.

Not quite, though. In Francis, Hunston and Manning we find 39 patterns of the 'N *of* n' class. They are distinguished by the different groups of head nouns that precede the *of*-phrases. In one of these groups, the 'love' group, we find *hatred*. This group comprises the nouns *admiration, approval, dislike, fear, hatred, hope, horror, love*. We are also given an explanation: "The noun refers to an attitude or feeling. The noun group after *of* indicates the thing or person that the attitude or feeling concerns" (Francis, Hunston & Manning 1998:180). Other groups of 'N *of* n' mean, it seems, different things. The 'architect' group, for instance, includes nouns such as *author, breeder, father*, and *pioneer*. This is its description: "These nouns refer to people who have created or founded something. The noun group after *of* indicates what the person created" (ibid.: 193). Still another group is the 'stage' group. Here the "noun refers to an aspect or part of something abstract". Nouns are, among many others, *aspect* [*every aspect of his life*], *basics, bottom, eve, middle, subsidiary, top* and *wreckage* (ibid.: 192). What is common to these groups in terms of their meaning, we may ask?

Our noun, *hatred*, is a member of five groups. We find it in the 'dismay' group of the 'poss N' class. "These nouns refer to particular feelings. With many of these nouns, the noun is usually or sometimes followed by a prepositional phrase". Nouns belonging here are, for instance, *approval, chagrin, displeasure* [*his displeasure at his team's over-physical approach*], *hatred, love, spleen* (ibid.: 72).

Another group in which we find *hatred* is the 'love' and 'enmity' group, part of the 'N *between* pl n' class. "These nouns refer to feelings that two or more people have towards each other". An example is *the extraordinary chemistry between Ingrid and Bogart* (ibid. 144). The next group is the 'love' and 'hatred' group, part of the 'N *for* n' class. "These nouns refer to feelings and attitudes. The prepositional phrase indicates who or what the feeling or attitude relates to". An example is *their hatred for one another* (p. 149). The fifth group is the 'hatred' group, part of the 'N *towards* n' class. "These nouns refer to attitudes and feelings. Most of them refer to specific attitudes or feelings, but *approach, attitude, feelings, line, policy* and *stance* are more general." An example is *We harbour no hatred towards you* (p. 227).

From a semantic (and perhaps also from a functional) perspective there seems to be some undeniable similarity between *hatred+of*-phrase, *hatred+for*-phrase and *hatred+towards*-phrase. This similarity is not discussed, however. Neither do we find a discussion of the (at least) two readings of the *hatred+of*-phrase: *their hatred of the French colonials* and the *hatred of the French colonials for the local population*. It cannot be discussed without an appropriate grammatical theory, something that, as cited above, Hunston and Francis would regard as "futile". In the next section I present an alternative model for coping with lexicogrammar, the Continental model of valency and dependency. This model would, I believe, have solutions for the problems of ambiguity and similarity and thus could augment the pattern grammar as we find it now.

My criticisms should not detract from the vast achievement of the *Grammar Patterns*. The aim of this undertaking is not to provide a grammatical analysis of the lexicogrammatical patterns we find in the corpus, but merely to present them. In this sense, we can view these patterns as ready-mades, as instantiations of Sinclair's co-selection principle, and not as grammatical structures whose internal workings need to be explored. There can be no doubt that the patterns, in the sheer inexhaustible thoroughness in which they have been extracted, are a novel and immensely welcome tool for any learner of English. My concern is that for the expert, e.g. for the language teacher, no presentation of evidence can be complete without an explanation and interpretation. For any presentation of patterns has to be based on categorisations. While these may remain implicit for the lay user, they need to be made explicit for fellow grammarians. Only then the new approach of pattern grammar can be given the attention it deserves.

4.   Categories and classifications in valency and dependency grammar

4.1 Operations

There are two key operations that help categorising and classifying the evidence the corpus gives us. These operations tell us, in the Saussurean sense, what can be grouped together and what stands in opposition towards each other. Without applying such operations in an explicit way, all our groupings appear to be made solely on the basis of surface similarity and intuition. Similarity, however, lies primarily in the eye of the beholder, and intuition is neither innate nor universal. Our goal is, however, to achieve a common understanding among linguists. This can only be achieved by relying on operations that can be reconstructed by other members of the community.

It would be wrong, I believe, to attribute too much to Sinclair's denunciation of the key operation that has been used by linguists over hundreds of years, the substitution test. His statement apropos the phrase *the city of York* should be taken cum grano salis: "Using the hallowed criterion of substitutability ... it defines *of* in this sense as *that is/are; being*. It is difficult to imagine in what circumstances a person will need this information" (Sinclair 1991:82). But is there really only one reading of the phrase *the city of York*? Could not have been there, in a feudal past, a person called York whose city had won the first prize in a beauty contest? The substitution test would distinguish between the two readings. In the second reading, we can replace *the city of York* with *the city which is somehow related to York*. No, I see Sinclair's statement, first of all, as an expression of his iconoclasm. All these years his message has been that we should always be wary of the ancient recipes and use them only if we cannot come up with something better, while on the other hand, as we have seen, he also warns of introducing novelties without good cause. So even if we need the substitution test, this does not absolve us from reflecting why we are using it and what it is we hope to achieve.

The substitution test gives us paradigms, paradigms of elements which can stand for each other according to an aspect that needs to be specified. This aspect could be merely syntactic (e.g. exchanging one element of the noun class by another element) or it could be meaning. Whatever we find impossible to put into the same paradigm, be it for syntactic or, as in this case, for semantic reasons, indicates an opposition that has to be dealt with: *the city owned by York* and *the city that is York* do not belong into the same category.

In a similar way, it would appear to be possible, for semantic purposes, to group together the examples *his hatred of the colonial French* and *his hatred for the colonial French*. On the first glance, the meaning of the two phrases is more or less identical. Yet after scanning hundreds of citations of *hatred+of*-phrase, and of *hatred+for*-phrase, I am not so sure any more. Somehow they have a different ring. Perhaps biased by my past spent on German grammar, I venture to suggest that *his hatred of the colonial French* expresses more of a long-lasting disposition which can well slumber for many years. *His hatred for the colonial French*, on the other hand, seems to call for more speedy action. The philologists taught us that many nominalizations such as *hatred* can be used both as 'nomina acti', also called 'nomina resultativum', and as 'nomen actionis'. I have to leave open here whether such an opposition would make sense for our example, and whether we would also want to distinguish between these phrases and *his hatred against the colonial French* or *his hatred towards the colonial French*.

Sinclair, I believe, wants to warn us that the substitution test (which is referred to as 'commutation' (in the mathematical sense) among valency linguists) does not provide us with groupings inherent to language. But in my view the categorisation and classification work of the grammarian does not 'discover' 'real' properties of a language. Rather we have to take all these categories and classes as inventions, as instruments, that help us to make useful distinctions. It is the community of grammarians that have the last word on this usefulness. Their views may change. That is why grammatical categories and classes are always provisional.

In the BNC, there is a citation of a *hatred+at*-phrase:

> Athelstan glimpsed red, dirty faces, greasy, matted hair, and the occasional glare of hatred at their well-fed horses and warm, woollen cloaks.

Is the *at*-phrase just another way of referring to the object of *hatred*? Substitutability by itself will not give us an answer. We have to explore other options. Is the phrase *at their well-fed horses* truly modifying *hatred* (which would seem strange to native speakers), or could it also be a phrase belonging to something else? Could it be a modifier of *glare*? Could one move the phrase directly to the right of *glare*, by dropping *of hatred* for the moment? Can one say *the occasional glare at their well-fed horses*? The corpus provides ample evidence that this indeed is possible, e.g.: *With a final glare at Yanto, he scrambled back up the bank*. The operation of substitution tells us that *glare*, rather than *hatred*, seems to be the head of the modifier *at their well-fed horses*.

Shifting phrases around in the sentence is the second key operation that grammarians can use. It is called permutation. I have to admit that it works much better for German, with its liberal word order, than for English. But we can make it work for English, as well, as I will show in the next section. Permutation does not work on the paradigmatic but on the syntagmatic dimension of language. It operates on the linearity of the sentence. Each sentence consists of a linear concatenation of words and phrases. The order is not random. There are structural constraints. By moving words and phrases around in sentences, we can learn about the boundaries of phrases, and their relationship towards each other. This is the operation that is called permutation in the valency/dependency grammar community.

Permutation and commutation are, unlike intuition and the idea of similarity, operations that others can reconstruct. Thus the categories and classes they suggest become negotiable. Prudently applied, they can help telling us what belongs to general grammar and what is the local grammar of a word that has to be dealt with in the dictionary.

4.2 Dependency grammar and its categories

The grammar of phrase structure, or of constituent structure, describes sentence structure in a hierarchy of levels. The top level is the sentence itself (S). It divides into the subject noun phrase (NP) and the verb phrase (VP). The verb phrase contains the constituents of the verb group itself (the main verb, plus modals and/or auxiliaries), and the object phrases, either NPs or prepositional phrases (PPs), or perhaps adverbial phrases. There can also be sentence adverbials, direct constituents of the S node. Noun phrases consist of the noun itself (N) plus determiners plus prenominal and postnominal modifiers, such as adjectives and PPs.

Dependency grammar takes the verb group to be the top node. The verb group consists, in principle, of the main verb plus modals and auxiliaries. On it depend the subject and the objects, both called complements. (It should be pointed out here that the complement of valency grammar is not what 'complement' means in pattern grammar, namely "a part of a clause that provides information about the person or thing indicated by the Subject [and typically following] a link verb" (Francis, Hunston & Manning 1998:xiv).) On the verb group depend also adjuncts, all those phrases that are neither (part of the) subject or (part of an) object but that are seen to relate to the verb group directly, including sentence adverbs. Complements and adjuncts come in various forms, often as noun phrases, sometimes as clauses, sometimes as pronouns or as adverbs or adverbial phrases. A very important category is the category of 'Satzglied', perhaps best translated as 'clause constituent'. All complements and adjuncts, regardless of their form, count as 'Satzglieder'. Nouns (and some adjectives) can be modified, for instance by adjectives, by other noun phrases or by prepositional phrases, or by clauses, e.g. by relative clauses or, in some cases, by *wh*-clauses. All these modifiers are called 'Attribute'. The operations commutation and permutation described above help us to distinguish 'Satzglieder', verb-dependent phrases, from 'Attribute', in my context: noun-dependent phrases. Why do we need such a distinction?

One of the *hatred* groups in the pattern grammar is the *hatred+for*-phrase, classified, as shown above, as the 'love' and 'hatred' group, part of the 'N *for* n' class. The preposition *for* is especially tricky, due to its fuzziness which invites often a variety of syntactic interpretations. Examples in the BNC in which *for* can be, but does not have to be, interpreted as expressing a relationship between *hatred* and the 'Attribut' expressing the object of *hatred* (and which would thus be equivalent to the 'love' and 'hatred' group in Francis, Hunston and Manning (1998)) are:

> Save all that fine, lusty hatred for me.
> Joyce had a special hatred for history.
> I felt no hatred for him.

These citations, as well as many of the 54 other citations (in the BNC) for *hatred for* can be interpreted in two ways. Either the *for*-phrase is, as Francis, Hunston and Manning (1998) claim, a modifier of *hatred*, or it is a complement dependent on the verb, or, in case the verb is not autonomous but just a support verb, on the lexical item functioning as a verb. Substitution by a pronoun yields, e.g., *Save it for me*, and *Save it, I felt nothing for him*, and *I didn't feel it*. Admittedly, there are a handful of clear cases, such as:

> It was a rural phenomenon, an aspect of peasant hatred for urban civilization.

For the language learner, the two alternative interpretations may not make much of a difference. But what do we do with sentences like these?

> It earned him their hatred for many years.
> They store up their hatred for release in an act of revenge.

While the surface structure is identical to the examples above, the *for*-phrases obviously do not depend on *hatred*. Again we become aware that the relationship established by *for* can be interpreted in different ways. The permutation operation gives us: *For many years it earned him their hatred* and *They store it up for release in an act of revenge*. Thus they are not 'Attribute', noun-dependent modifiers, to *hatred*, but 'Satzglieder', phrases depending directly on the verb. In the first case, it is an adjunct referring to a temporal entity, in the second case I would call it a complement (or maybe an adjunct) indicating a purpose. This is a distinction that language learners have to make consciously. The categories 'Satzglied' and 'Attribut' are essential when it comes to describing syntactic structure. Not everything that looks like 'N *for* n', in the terminology of Francis, Hunston and Manning (1998) is really 'N *for* n'.

4.3 Complements and adjuncts

Valency theory aims to distinguish what is part of the general grammar from the local grammar of a word or a (more or less) fixed expression. It investigates whether and how the lexical item in question interacts with other lexical items within the clause or the sentence. Those interactions that are specific to a lexical item have to be dealt with in the dictionary. They belong to lexicogrammar. Relationships that any element of a word class, of a part of speech, a noun, for instance, can establish with other lexical items do not have to be treated in the dictionary. To a certain extent, this has been the custom for a considerable time. Some nouns, unlike *hatred*, are countable. We find this information in the dictionary because I have to know whether I can put a definite and, in particular, an indefinite article in front of it (and also whether I can put the noun in the plural). But the dictionary does not tell us whether I can modify the noun with an adjective or a relative clause. As this can be done, in principle, with any noun, there is no need to mention it specifically in the dictionary.

For our example, *hatred*, our question is to which categories the prepositional phrases belong that we have been looking at. Francis, Hunston and Manning list four: *between, for, of* and *towards*. But there are more. In alphabetical order, we find right-adjacent of *hatred* (under exclusion of those which depend not on *hatred* but on a different lexical item):

> such a particular hatred **against** the lord Isambard
> three gypsies aroused much hatred **among** the Rouennais
> this sparked off new hatred **amongst** the peasants
> he saw Simon's eyes gleam with hatred **at** him.
> suspicion, contempt and even downright hatred **between** the two countries
> save all that fine, lusty hatred **for** me
> the hatred **in** her voice had shocked him
> an attack motivated by the hatred **of** the past
> it's not seen as hatred **to** women
> my hatred **towards** those who oppressed me
> the memory strengthened the hatred **within** her

Francis, Hunston and Manning make no claim of completeness. There are only a handful of occurrences of *hatred against* which one therefore might be justified to ignore. The citation for *hatred to* belongs to spoken language, is unique and is not worth our attention. If we accept the *at*-phrase cited as dependent on *hatred* we can still dismiss it as too infrequent.

More interesting is, I think, the fact Francis, Hunston and Manning do not mention *hatred* in connection with *among(st)*, *in* and *within*. The last one is rare indeed, but the others come up frequently enough. Let us have a closer look at *hatred in*. There are 32 occurrences in the BNC. About 18 to 22 occurrences of these *in*-phrases can be said to be not dependent on *hatred* (some citations allow both readings), e.g.:

> And he had **seen** hatred *in those eyes*.
> There **was** hatred *in his voice* now.

Our commutation/permutation operations yield *In those eyes, he had seen hatred*, and *In his voice now, there was hatred*. In these cases, it is advisable to interpret the prepositional phrase as dependent on *was* or *seen*, respectively. In the other citations, i.e. at least ten, *hatred* depends definitely on the noun. Here are a few examples:

> She flashed her eyes up at him, **hatred** *in their depths*.
> A man thrust past, dragging another, and stopped and lifted his axe, **hatred** *in his face*.
> Isabel shivered at the implacable **hatred** *in Matilda's voice*.
> But that **hatred** *in that dream*.
> She was like a hag: all youthful beauty banished below the lines and **hatred** *in her face*.
> Corbett, surprised by malicious **hatred** *in the woman's eyes*, hurriedly stepped away.

The citations make us aware of a certain semantic preference. The prepositional phrase features, to a significant extent, eyes, voices and faces. For an investigation into the formulaic aspect of language this would be a relevant finding. Here, however, we are concerned with grammar. From this perspective we have to note that *in*-phrases can, in principle, depend on all nouns. They are, however, specific to a certain subset of nouns, a subset of which *hatred*, but not, for instance, *table*, would be an element.

Here are some examples of noun-dependent *in*-phrases, taken from the BNC:

> The second **weakness** *in the Government's position* is that it is ambiguous.
> This should suggest that further **work** *in a variety of sub-disciplines* be carried out here.
> This represents only the most recent **episode** *in a history stretching back to the Mesozoic*.

Following their **success** _in a Dubai tournament_ _in November_, the Scots have been
seeded first for an event in Canberra.
Our **policies** _in the epoch of so-called war communism_ could not be aimed at developing the productive forces.
A comparison of **social product** per head _in the 1950s_ with that _in 1986_ (_in current
dinars_, unadjusted for regional **differences** _in the cost of living_) shows a significant
improvement for Montenegro.
A party with a commitment to **change** _in the institutional form of the market_
would never get elected.

As we can see, there is a wide spectrum of _in_-phrases. Some are spatial, some are
temporal, some are abstract. Leaving aside the abstract ones (because they are ex-
cruciatingly complex to deal with) I look here at the spatial and temporal ones.
They can be grouped together on the basis of the commutation operation, for they
all commute with other prepositional phrases of a comparable spatial or temporal meaning. Which preposition is chosen does not depend on the head noun on
which the prepositional phrase depends but on the internal requirements of the
prepositional phrase. Thus we find (my examples):

our **policies** _in the epoch_ / _on Friday mornings_ / _during the election_ / _after the events_
their **success** _in a tournament_ / _on the lawn_ / _under his presidency_ / _at the competi-
tion_
the **social product** _in dinars_ /_in 1957_ / _on the average_ / _north of the Danube_ / _since
the election_
the **differences** _over the years_ / _between the countries_ / _within the sample_ / _in eye-
colour_ / _on this floor_

In valency theory, we call phrases (i.e. 'Satzglieder') and subphrasal units (modifiers of nouns, adjectives and adverbs, (i.e. 'Attribute')) that can come with any
element of the given part of speech, but that do not have to be there, 'adjuncts'.
The rules concerning adjuncts are rules belonging to general grammar. The information which adjuncts can depend on a noun is not needed in the dictionary.
It would have to be repeated for every noun there is. While adjuncts depend on
verbs, nouns, adjectives and adverbs, they do not have to be described in the local
grammar of any of them.

This is, I believe, the reason why we do not find them in Francis, Hunston and
Manning. It shows they are aware of the adjunct/complement distinction, but they
do not refer to it in explicit terms.

Complements, on the other hand, are the very essence of local grammar.
Noun-dependent complements are those modifiers which occur only with a given
sub-class of nouns. But how can we define these subclasses? Francis, Hunston and
Manning attempt what I would call intensional definitions by identifying groups

of nouns that share certain semantic properties. Even though they do not explicitly advise users who are looking for a word not listed, it is understood that it will
behave like the words whose semantic features it shares. After all, the rationale of
pattern grammar is to show that syntactic structure is closely associated to meaning. Yet my analysis of German nominal valency (Teubert 1979) came to the conclusion that semantic features can be a meretricious guide for the local grammar
of a noun.

The relationship between a complement and the noun it depends on has, of
course, a semantic dimension, independent of the semantic features of these nouns.
Case grammar, whether as the Fillmore original or in any other guise, has worked
hard to explore it. However, the arbitrariness of the classification has given cause
to much discontent. I do not think these deep cases are useless. But they have to
be closely linked to grammatical features. Complement classes and adjunct classes
provide the necessary interface between the semantic and the syntactic dimension
of these relationships.

4.4 Complement and adjunct classes

So far I have mentioned a number of noun-dependent complement and adjunct
classes. Complements are gen.subi., gen.obi., gen.expl., and gen.part. I left open the
question how to classify the *against*-phrases, *for*-phrases and the *towards*-phrases
that complement *hatred*. This is the time to remind ourselves that these classes
are to be negotiated by the grammarians, and that any agreement will depend on
the objective of the investigation. In the case of *hatred*, it seems to make sense to
group them together, and to include into this grouping even the *of*-phrases (which
we have classified as gen.obi. realisations). After all, *hatred* is derived from the verb
hate, and *hate* has only one direct object. Thus, there should be only one complement class for the complement of *hatred* (which is equivalent to the complement
commonly called the direct object of *hate*), and if we define it in analogy to the
verb complement, all the relevant different surface realisations should be grouped
together as gen.obi.

Why do we need these complement classes at all? The same surface realisations we find e.g., for gen.obi., we can also find as realisation of other complement
or adjunct classes. Take for instance this phrase: *Tuesday's murder of a Catholic
father of five*. In most cases, the premodifying possessive stands for a gen.subi. (It
should be noted here that for Francis, Hunston and Manning (1998:xv), the possessive is also what "comes after the noun [in] the form of a prepositional phrase
beginning with *of*". In this paper, however, 'poss', the possessive, refers only to what
precedes the head noun.) Not in this case, though. Here it tells us when the murder

occurred. Actually not quite; what it tells us is that *Tuesday* stands in some un-specified relationship to *murder*, and it is up to the speaker/hearer to give an in-terpretation to this relationship. This is the genitivus possessivus (gen.poss.), an adjunct class. It can occur with any noun, not just with nominalizations. We can even speak about *Tuesday's table* or *Tuesday's university* when we want to identify the table we saw in the shop on Tuesday, or the university we visited on Tuesday. Similarly, we could talk about *this university's murders*, i.e. the murders that oc-curred at this university, or about *Rome's tables*, e.g. if we want to compare them to the tables they had in Athens. This unspecified relationship between two concrete or abstract objects is the essence of the adjunct class of genitivus possessivus. We need it if we want to make sense out of these lines in Gilbert and Sullivan's opera *The Pirates of Penzance*:

> With the estate, I bought the chapel and the ancestors it contains. I don't know whose ancestors they were, but I know whose ancestors they are now.

The joke here resides in the phrase *whose ancestors*. In the first occurrence of *an-cestors*, it refers to the former owners of the chapel who had the people they de-scended from buried there. This is what I would suggest to call a genitive of speci-fied interpersonal relations (gen.s.i.r.). We find it with kinship terms, but also with, e.g., *teacher, doctor, sister, supervisee* etc. In the second occurrence the relationship between *whose* and *ancestors* is unspecified, and it is only the context that tells us that it is a relationship of private property. This, then, would count as an instance of a gen.poss.

We need complement (and adjunct) classes to distinguish what looks structur-ally alike on the surface but needs to be separated (by commutation and permuta-tion operations) to allow the appropriate reading. This is blatantly obvious for the distinction between gen.subi. and gen.obi. In most instances, we find a gen.obi. realised as an *of*-phrase (or as another prepositional phrase), while the gen.subi. complement is frequently realised as a possessive. But there are a number of nouns which allow gen.obi. complements to be realised as possessives and there are also a number of nouns which allow gen.subi. complements to be realised as *of*-phrases. Let us take, for instance, first some examples of poss. for gen.subi. and gen. obi, with *murder* as head noun:

> (gen.subi.) Uther Pendragon's lust for Igraine, *his* **murder** of Gorlais, his seduc-tion of Igraine and her subsequent giving birth to Arthur form the basis of the Arthurian legend!

> (gen.obi.) For if Mrs Phipps been clever enough to manage *her husband's* **murder**, then she was too bright to make such uninhibited admissions, even to a sympa-thetic vicar's wife, other than in the knowledge that she'd nothing to hide.

Here are examples for gen.subi. and gen.obi. realised as *of*-phrases, with *hatred* as head noun:

> (gen.subi.) All power, all profits, all our sources of livelihood are in their hands: but the one thing they leave behind will destroy them: the **hatred** *of a million coolies!*

> (gen.obi.) Their **hatred** *of Wilson* and their determination to undermine him had become legendary and earned him support in unexpected places.

Complement classes are specific for subclasses of nouns. A gen.s.i.r. cannot depend on all nouns but only on nouns implying some kind of specified relationship with another (group of) person(s). It is the complement classes which determine the local grammar of a noun. Adjunct classes are not specific for subclasses. An adjunct such as gen.poss. can, in principle, depend on any noun. Adjunct classes belong to general grammar. Complement and adjunct classes are constructs needed for the disambiguation of identical syntactic surface structures. They provide the interface between the meaning (not of the head noun but) of the relationship that obtains between the head noun and the complement or adjunct in question and the syntactic realisation of this complement or adjunct. In most cases, there are different ways in which complements and adjuncts can be realised syntactically.

4.5 The syntactic realisation of complements

We need complement and adjunct classes to detect oppositions in surface structures that look identical from a syntactic perspective. But how can we link these surface structures to the relevant complement classes? (For reasons of brevity, I will leave out adjunct classes here. Their relationship with syntactic surface structure is, on the whole, more straightforward than that between complement classes and their realisations.) As we will see, general rules give only a general frame of what we actually find. We can say that a gen.subi. can be syntactically realised by a possessive, by an *of*-phrase and by a *by*-phrase, to mention the three most common realisations. However, it depends on the noun in question (in addition to other constraints) which of these three options are available. In many cases, we also have to distinguish between the singular and the plural. While *His murder was executed beautifully* can be read as gen.subi. and as gen.obi., *His murders all were carried out beautifully* can, for obvious reasons, only be a gen.subi. Thus the possible syntactic realisations are, again, part of the local grammar. General grammar will not tell us whether an *of*-phrase depending on the noun *invitation* can be read as gen.subi, gen.obi. or both.

These are, according to our corpus, the BNC, the realisations of the gen.subi. and gen.obi. for *invitation(s)*:

gen.subi. sg

(poss.) He wanted her to accept the *Hamiltons'* **invitation**.

(*of*-phrase) AI visited Bhutan in January at the **invitation** *of King Jigme Wang-chuck.*

(*by*-phrase, very rare) The **invitation** *by the BDDA* to these distinguished brothers reflected the respect for the achievements of the American deaf-mutes.

gen.subi. pl.

(poss.) *Her* **invitations** to colleagues to define their terms often disconcert the unprepared.

(*of*-phrase, very rare) Adonis, cold and puritanical, rejects the lustful **invitations** *of Venus.*

(*by*-phrase, very rare) Personal handwritten **invitations** *by the class involved to their own parents* will pull in a few more adults.

gen.obi. sg.

(poss.) no occurrence

(*of*-phrase) no occurrence

(*for*-phrase, rare) It must include an **invitation** *for readers* to get full written details of the terms.

(*to*-phrase, very rare) He went back with a formal **invitation** *to James III and VII* to reclaim his kingdom.

gen.obi. pl.

(poss.) no occurrence

(*of*-phrase) no occurrence

(*for*-phrase, very rare) It wasn't long before even the sporadic **invitations** *for his son* to holiday in the States petered out altogether.

(*to*-phrase, very rare) Official **invitations** *to all les Girls* would be pinned up on the stage doorkeeper's noticeboard.

It seems to be somewhat odd to use the label gen.obi. if the realisations of what corresponds to the direct object of *invite* are not *of*-phrases but other prepositional phrases. As Sinclair pointed out, *of*-phrases should, for syntactic reasons, be kept separate from prepositional phrases (1991:86). Grouping noun-dependent complements in a specific group is always arbitrary and had to be justified. It will ultimately depend on the purpose of such a classification how we define the categories, both in intensional and extensional terms.

Also, it should be mentioned that we frequently find in complementary distribution to the realisation of a gen.subi. complement the complement class 'direction', realised as a *from*-phrase, which confronts us again with having to decide whether they should be grouped together or not:

> Art lived alone now and welcomed the **invitations** *from his eldest son Toby and his wife Lynn.*

Finally, it should be observed that the gen.obi. realised as a *to*-phrase is in opposition to another complement 'theme', also realised as a *to*-phrase:

> **Invitations** *to these seminars* have been sent to centres intending to participate.

There are no general rules, not even rules of the thumb, that would tell us in which ways a complement class such as gen.obi. can be realised for a given noun. We may agree that the *towards*-phrase (as we encountered it above depending on *hatred*) can be classified as a gen.obi. But it has to be established for noun after noun belonging to the noun subclass of gen.obi. whether this realisation is possible. The semantic features of these nouns would be a very poor indicator. A standard thesaurus offers, among others, these synonyms for *hatred*: *dislike, grudge, disgust, loathing, repugnance, hostility.* Antonyms, and therefore also relevant, would be *love, fondness, adoration.* Which of them can realise the gen.obi. as a *towards*-phrase? This is the corpus evidence:

> ***dislike towards***: no hit
> ***grudge towards***: no hit
> ***disgust towards***: 1 (wrong) hit — The person should be **directing** their disgust *towards those people* who inflict these atrocities on defenceless foxes.
> ***loathing towards***: no hit
> ***repugnance towards***: 2 hits — Many couples have experienced a **repugnance** *towards sex* with no apparent reason.
> ***hostility towards***: 117 hits — Also there is more **hostility** *towards academics* than in Holland.
> ***love towards***: 11 hits — After ten sessions mother shows **love** *towards the child.*
> ***fondness towards***: no hit
> ***adoration towards***: no hit

Discounting *disgust* for syntactic reasons, we are left with only three out of nine semantically similar words which allow *towards*-phrases. In addition, the rarity of this syntactic realisation depending on *repugnance* and *love* makes them appear like borderline cases.

Francis, Hunston and Manning list seven semantically categorised groups of nouns featuring a *towards*-phrase. One is the 'hatred' group, which I referred to above. It is fairly obvious that the semantic features the nouns listed for a particular syntactically defined group share cannot necessarily be generalised. This is also true for the 'tendency' group, characterised thus: "These nouns refer to a tendency or a desire to do, be, or have a particular thing". Six nouns are listed: *impulse, inclination, leaning, orientation, predisposition, tendency* (Francis, Hunston &

Manning 1998:228). These are some of the synonyms of *tendency* we would find in a standard thesaurus: *readiness, trend, drift, course, proneness, bent*. This is what the corpus tells us:

> *readiness* (592 occurrences; no hit)
> *trend* (2612; 282 hits): The **trend** *towards consolidation* slowed down somewhat in the 1970s.
> *drift* (1249; 52 hits (including verbs)): Alderson has had the temerity to caution the service about an apparent **drift** *towards paramilitarism*.
> *course* (48,992; 10 hits): We shall follow his change of **course** *towards religious belief* in the next section.
> *proneness* (11): no hit
> *bent* (only nouns: 30): no hit

The result again tells us not to rely on the semantic features of a word if we want to make an informed guess about its syntactic pattern(s). If we discount *course towards* due to its relative rarity, there are just two out of six synonyms that allow the *towards*-phrase as the syntactic realisation of a 'theme' complement. But are the words cited really synonyms of *tendency*? Should we not rule out those words as synonyms which display a deviant syntactic behaviour, mindful of the basic assumption of pattern grammar that syntactic form and meaning are closely associated? I do not think so, and neither would, I believe, Sinclair. His recent proposals for a new kind of thesaurus excludes syntactic features, even the category of part of speech. Instead, the words are grouped together according to the hypernym they have in common in their respective defining sentences. Thus we would find *pep talk, declamatory*, and *swagger* all in the same group of hyponyms for *confident*. For all the synonyms cited above we could well imagine defining sentences using *tendency* as hypernym (Sinclair 2004:438f.).

If we need the complement classes for distinguishing between identical syntactic surface structures with different meanings, we have also to know, for each noun on which complements depend, how these complements are syntactically realised. This knowledge is not readily available. But it is what language learners should find in their dictionaries.

4.6 The three-level approach

To describe the working of prepositional phrases depending on nouns we need a three-level approach. There is a top level listing, in semantic terms, the relationships obtaining between the head noun and the dependent phrases. This classification is based on expedience. It is something to be negotiated by linguists, not to be discovered. We find it exemplified in the multitude of case grammar proposals floating around since Fillmore's paper on semantic cases. It will posit only those classes needed to distinguish whatever we find opposed to each other, in a syntactic or semantic way. On this level, the classification is still language-independent. It should work for Chinese, Japanese and for Russian equally well. We need this level to interpret, in semantic terms, the relationship between a noun and the phrases that depend on it.

There are arguments that the complement/adjunct distinction does not make sense for all languages, for instance for Hungarian. So we may do well to assign this distinction to a middle level, a level that interacts between semantics and syntax. This is the level of the complement and adjunct classes. From above, they are defined by their association to semantically determined deep cases. From below, they are defined by their association with the set of syntactic realisations that we find for them. We need this level in order to distinguish between syntactically identical surface structures whose semantic interpretation is ambiguous.

Finally we need the level of syntactic realisations. It tells us, for every noun, how the complement classes that it allows can be syntactically realised. This is the level that is foregrounded by pattern grammar. But in my opinion it only can be put to use if the syntactic realisations are firmly linked to the complement classes they represent.

5. Conclusion

Pattern grammar and valency grammar are both born out of the understanding that we need a link between lexis and general grammar. Lexical items, however complex they may be internally, cannot simply be concatenated without grammatical considerations. For just as lexical items are units of meaning, the relationships obtaining between them also carry meaning. What is needed therefore is a lexical grammar that tells us which syntactic surface structure to the left and to the right of a lexical item carries which relational meaning.

I think the present paper has made it clear that there is no reason to unquestioningly accept the categories traditional grammar provides us with. We do not need linguistic examples that match the venerable categories borrowed from Latin grammar; we need categories that help us to detect and describe the distinctions that real language data confront us with. Does it make sense to call the noun-dependent complement corresponding to the direct object in verbs gen.obi. even in cases in which it cannot be syntactically realised, as with *invitation*, as an *of*-phrase? Do we need subtler semantic distinctions than we find, for instance, in the case of Fillmore's 'goal' case? The answer must, in each case, depend on the goal of our investigation.

This paper deals with the question whether patterns can replace syntax. My aim was to show that the relationship between grammar and meaning is more complex than the language user (as native speaker or as language learner) is aware of. But while the native speaker can trust his or her 'instinct', the learners must be told what they can say and what it means. While I agree with Sinclair and his collaborators that the traditional rule-based approach to grammar will never do, we may disagree on how much complexity we need for describing the grammar/meaning relationship. No doubt much of what we see can be explained in terms of analogy, and pattern grammar seems to test how far analogy can go. But the relationship between grammar and meaning is equally determined by anomaly. Analogy goes together with language awareness and an intuition of what can be said and what cannot be said. It is the native speaker's refuge. Language learners have to fight against anomalies. Anomalies can only be treated in lists. The list-based approach, the dictionary approach, indeed resolves the analogy/anomaly opposition by providing all the information needed, be it reducible to analogy, or be it exceptional.

I do think that Sinclair, who always insists that the linguist has expert knowledge not needed by the language user, be they native speakers or language learners, would not talk about grammar as competently as he does without at least implicitly applying classifications and categories. His review of the *Longman Grammar* makes this more than clear. This is, of course, also the case for Gill Francis, Susan Hunston and Elizabeth Manning. Michael Halliday has put it into these words: "[T]hey make considerable use of grammatical categories…What they are doing is medium delicacy grammar, setting up grammatical classes 'on the basis of their behaviour' and giving them names…[W]hat they are doing is to enrich the entire panorama of the lexicogrammar by revealing systematic patterns at a greater degree of delicacy than had been recognized hitherto" (Halliday 2002:15 f.).

It seems in the end that the Continental and the British approach are not so far apart. Valency grammar and pattern grammar may have different origins, but they are born out of the same aporia that traditional grammar presents, and they both strive to provide the long missing link between grammar and lexis. John Sinclair and his collaborators have begun to bridge the gap between grammatology and lexicology, a gap that has been left open even by Michael Halliday. Even if pattern grammar cannot do altogether away with the traditional operations of grammatical analysis, it is a necessary, if not entirely sufficient, step to arrive at an integration of grammar and the lexicon. "John Sinclair … is one of the most theoretically-minded linguists I know", says Halliday (2002:18), and right he is.

Little of what we, the speakers, and we, the linguists, say can lay much claim to originality. What sounds new can almost always be broken down into smaller units that have populated our discourses for a long time. Our utterances consist overwhelmingly of prefabricated building blocks we select from a discourse to construct new meaning. How can we express our creativity in such a system of fixed rules? In his last book, *Linear Unit Grammar*, co-authored with Anna Mauranen, John Sinclair has expanded on his earlier ideas on grammatical patterning, or chunking. Exocentric constructions consist of more than one chunk and express relations such as "subject/predicate, verb/object, preposition/noun phrase". An exocentric construction is a textual incident, and as such it "updates the virtual world and changes it". Endocentric constructions, however, are single chunks, realisations of existing patterns, the building blocks of all utterances, and any attempt to break their structure up would destroy them (see Sinclair/Mauranen 2006:149).

Together, the noun *hatred*, embedded in an endocentric construction, for instance in the chunk *such a particular hatred*, and the chunk that modifies it, for instance *against the lord Isambard*, form an exocentric construction. If I want to describe the relationship between the two chunks, I do well to commute it into a sentence like *someone hates the lord Isambard in a particular way*. Valency grammar provides, in form of tests such as substitution, commutation and permutation, procedures for classifying the contingent relationships between the chunks that exocentric constructions comprise. *Linear Unit Grammar* gives us a new and original perspective complementing, but not contradicting, grammatical traditions. It describes the tension between the parts of language that are fixed and those engaging our creativity. In what would become his last book, John has shown how we, the speakers, and we, the linguists, can be original without breaking up the consensus existing in our discourse communities.

References

B[ritish] N[ational] C[orpus]. www.natcorp.ox.ac.uk

Engel, U. (1977). *Syntax der deutschen Gegenwartssprache*. Berlin: E. Schmitt.

Fillmore, C. (1968). The case for case. In E. Bach & R. Harms (Eds.), *Universals in Linguistic Theory* (pp. 1–90). New York: Holt, Rinehart and Winston.

Francis, G. (1993). A corpus-driven approach to grammar: principles, methods and examples. In M. Baker, G. Francis & E. Tognini-Bonelli (Eds.) *Text and Technology: In Honour of John Sinclair* (pp.137–156). Amsterdam: John Benjamins.

Francis, G., Hunston, S. & Manning, E. (1998). *Grammar Patterns 2: Nouns and Adjectives*. London: HarperCollins.

Halliday, M. A. K. (2002). *"Judge Takes No CAP In Mid-Sentence": On the Complementarity of Grammar and Lexis.* The First Open Sinclair Lecture. Birmingham: The University of Birmingham, Department of English.

Hunston, S. & Francis, G. (1999). *Pattern Grammar.* Amsterdam: John Benjamins

Krishnamurthy, R. (2004). (Ed.) Sinclair, J. M., with Jones, S. & Daley, R., *English Collocation Studies: The OSTI Report.* London: Continuum Books.

Quirk, R., Greenbaum, S., Leech, G. & Svartvik, J. (1972). *A Grammar of Contemporary English.* London: Longman

Sinclair, J. M. (2004). To complement the dictionary. In R. Blatná & V. Petkevič (Eds.), *Jazyky a Jazykověda: Sborník k 65. narozeninám prof. PhDr. Františka Čermáka, DrSc.* (pp. 417–444). Prague: FFUK — ÚČNK.

Sinclair, J. M. (2001). Review of Biber et al. (1999), *Longman Grammar of Spoken and Written English. International Journal of Corpus Linguistics* 6(2), 339–359.

Sinclair, J. M. (1991). *Corpus, Concordance, Collocation.* Oxford: Oxford University Press.

Sinclair, J. M. (Ed.) (1990). *Collins COBUILD English Grammar.* London: HarperCollins.

Sinclair, J. M. & Mauranen, A. (2006). *Linear Unit Grammar.* Amsterdam: John Benjamins.

Teubert, W. (1979). *Valenz des Substantivs.* Düsseldorf: Schwann.

Semantic prosody revisited

Susan Hunston
University of Birmingham

This paper considers the contentious term 'semantic prosody' and discusses a number of aspects of the concept described by the term. It is pointed out that although many writers use it to refer to the implied attitudinal meaning of a word, Sinclair uses the term to refer to the discourse function of a unit of meaning. Problems of apparent counter-examples, when a word or unit does not have the semantic prosody that is typical of it, are discussed. The second point made is that the phenomena described as 'semantic prosody' can be regarded as observational data, but that they are often used to explain subjective reactions to a given text or to predict such reactions. The issues raised by these different uses are discussed. Finally, the pitfalls of using concordance lines to observe attitudinal language in highly opinionated texts are discussed.

Keywords: semantic prosody, unit of meaning, attitudinal language, intertextuality

1. Introduction

The term 'semantic prosody' was first used by Louw (1993) but attributed to Sinclair (1991) who developed the concept in later work (e.g. Sinclair 2004). The term has also been used by Stubbs (1996, 2001), Tognini-Bonelli (2001) and Partington (1998, 2004), among many others. It has also been strenuously criticised, for example by Whitsitt (2005). As a concept, it arises from corpus linguistics, and in particular the 'phraseological' tradition that focuses on the typical behaviour of individual lexical items as observed using 'key word in context' concordance lines (e.g. Sinclair 2003). Concordance lines reveal that many words occur frequently in recurring sequences, suggesting that large proportions of running text might be composed of semi-fixed 'chunks' (Sinclair 1991, 2004).

There are a number of potential sites of disagreement relating to differences in the way the concept of semantic prosody is used. Some of these might be summarised by considering the work of two proponents of semantic prosody: Sinclair (2004) and Partington (2004). Both take as their starting point the individual word (e.g. *budge* or *brook* for Sinclair, *happen* or *sheer* for Partington), and both stress the fact that meaning belongs to a unit that is larger than the word. Partington's discussion, however, prioritises semantic prosody as the property of a word, and as a feature that distinguishes near-synonyms, whereas Sinclair stresses that the word is only the core of a longer sequence of co-occurring items comprising a 'unit of meaning' of which semantic prosody is one of the identifying features. ('Word' should perhaps be in scare quotes as the core item may in fact be two, or more, words, as in *naked eye*.)

Secondly, whereas Partington associates semantic prosody explicitly with a binary distinction between positive and negative attitudinal meanings, Sinclair expresses difficulty in finding a specific characterisation for the semantic prosody, or attitudinal discourse function, of the various units of meaning he describes. Aside from in early work on items such as *set in*, semantic prosody is not described simply as 'good' or 'bad'. This difference leads to another. Partington regards semantic prosody as gradable: a word may have a 'more or less' favourable or unfavourable prosody depending on how frequently it occurs in good, bad or neutral contexts; whereas for Sinclair semantic prosody is an obligatory property of a unit of meaning, although it may be more or less explicit in any one example.

A final point of debate, and for Whitsitt (2005) the most contentious, is the extent to which semantic prosody 'carries over' from one context to another (see Hunston (2002:141) for a definition, following Louw, that depends on this point). Most simply put, it has been argued that if a lexical item most frequently occurs in a context of clearly positive or negative attitudinal meaning, then when it occurs in a different context that positive or negative meaning will colour the interpretation of the given instance. The result is that an additional attitudinal meaning, derived intertextually, is implied.

The purpose of this paper is to reconsider some of the phenomena often discussed under the heading 'semantic prosody' and in doing so to raise some more general issues relating to the interpretation of information from corpora. My aim is not so much to find a precise definition of 'semantic prosody' as to draw attention to some issues that surround observations of typical lexical behaviour.

2.   Semantic prosody: co-occurrence or discourse function?

As noted above, discussions of semantic prosody tend to focus on one of two types of consistency: (a) consistent co-occurrence of (types of) linguistic items (see Partington 2004) or (b) consistency in the discourse function of a sequence of such items (Sinclair 2004; cf. Stubbs on 'discourse prosody' (2001)). This section will consider both uses.

Consistency in the co-occurrence of items is often cited when the focus of attention is the behaviour of a word or of a short multi-word unit such as a phrasal verb. Well-known examples include Sinclair's study of *set in* (1991:73–74), Stubbs on *cause* (1995) and Louw on *utterly* (1993:160), among many others. In each case, the word or phrase is observed to co-occur frequently with a wide range of items that do not truly belong to a semantic set, but which have in common a particular attitudinal meaning (Partington 2004). This is illustrated in Figure 1, which shows a random selection of instances of the verb CAUSE.[1] The words indicating what entity is 'caused' in each line are highlighted in bold. In most cases (line 17 is an exception), this entity is one which would normally be considered to be undesirable: *confusion, a rift, anger, audience fragmentation, a kidney stone* and so on. It is sometimes said, then, that CAUSE 'has a negative (or unfavourable) semantic prosody', suggesting that an association with evaluatively negative things is a property of the verb.

```
1  a real downer of a word, likely to cause a lot of confusion. After
2    until I told her. What I did has caused a rift between me and my friend'
3  nd. His decision to oppose the war caused amazement in the ranks of SNP
4  quality in the borough". The award caused anger among anti-racist groups a
5    of new media outlets and choice, causing audience fragmentation. To achi
6  een suffering from a kidney stone, caused by excess build-up of urine. No
7  s chronic unemployment problem is caused by featherbedding workers with
8  de, Isle of Wight, last June which caused damage estimated at £100,000.
9                in some carrots could cause dizziness and vomiting, but said
10 control fairly rapidly. Hepatitis causes inflammation of the liver and ca
11 minority of individuals intent on causing misery to their neighbours. The
12 ews of the government's proposals caused outrage among medical associatio
13    issues, but it is starting to cause problems of supply. The traditio
14   of things in your life that are causing real concern. Don't be complete
15 se that her disappearance did not cause serious concern. The social
16    against the gynaecologist who caused so much unnecessary pain and mis
17   Saddam, journalism so strong it caused the West to liberate northern Ir
18        No one knows quite what caused this frenzy. The setting up of
```

Figure 1.

For the moment we will consider just two of the criticisms of this approach. One point to be made is that a word which is used in a certain way in most contexts is not necessarily used in that way in all contexts.[2] Figure 2, for example, shows twelve examples of CAUSE (each taken from the journal *New Scientist*) where no particular attitude can be discerned towards the entity brought into being, even when an extended context is shown. Evaluation is present in most examples, but what is evaluated is the respective researchers' success or difficulty in solving a particular research problem (see, for example, *the keys to the researchers' success* in 1 or *the chief practical problem* in 4). Identification of causation may help the research, but the thing caused is not in itself either desirable or undesirable.

1. *They [researchers] also searched for a second group of molecules called desensitisation proteins, which temporarily stop the receptor cells from responding to an odour.* **These proteins cause a smell to become less strong if we continue to sniff at it.** *The keys to the researchers' success were antibodies which recognise ...*

2. *When mounted a few micrometres above a chip, the probe and circuit form a capacitor.* **Any AC signal flowing beneath the probe causes a displacement current to flow through this capacitor.** *The value of this current changes depending on the amplitude and phase of the AC signal, enabling the signal to be imaged.*

3. *If signals are seen,* **how will we be certain that they are caused by dark matter particles?** *One way of finding out would be ...*

4. *Whatever their views about the causes of the more mysterious amphibian declines, herpetologists agree about one thing:* **the chief practical problem is distinguishing genuine, long-term changes in population trends from fluctuations caused by short-term variations in weather.**

5. *The astronomers found that a part of the absorption spectrum called the Lyman alpha line ... had been red-shifted by a factor of 3.390 so that it appeared at visible wavelengths.* **They knew that this Lyman alpha line was caused by a galaxy** *because it matched the equivalent line in a faint, visible galaxy near to the quasar.*

6. *Irwin speculates that those stars are young — only a few billion years old — because* **they formed in a burst of star formation caused by a tidal interaction with the Milky Way.**

7. *This lost cold air is replaced by the warmer air in the room which must subsequently be cooled when the door is closed again.* **The low specific heat and thermal conductivity of the filling will minimise the heat loss caused by convection while the door is open.** *... However, I suspect that the energy saved by filling an upright freezer with polystyrene foam is not significant.*

8. **INEL's system, which should be working by the end of next year, monitors changes in the Earth's magnetic field caused by metal objects passing through it.**

9. *But over hundreds of millions of years it [the star] loses mass in a stream of particles like the solar wind. This takes away angular momentum from the star, causing it to spin more slowly.*

10. *The behaviour of the tippe top can be described for the non-mathematician in fairly simple terms by reference to the diagram below.* **When the top is set spinning the low centre of mass causes the centre to be centrifugally displaced from the spin axis (Z),** *which remains perpendicular to the surface on which the top is spinning.*

11. *If hives of Cape bees are placed beside hives of African bees,* **the Cape bee infiltrates the African colonies causing the African bees to destroy each other.**

12. *The power the tides tap is the rotational energy of the Earth, relative to the Moon and Sun. The Moon orbits the Earth once a month, and the Earth spins on its axis once a day. The effect of the tides is like a brake, causing the spin of the Earth to slow while, to conserve angular momentum, accelerating the Moon to a higher orbit.*

Figure 2.

The obvious difference between the examples in Figure 1 and those in Figure 2 is that in Figure 1 the caused entities are either illnesses or symptoms (suffered by people), or emotions such as *anger, confusion, frenzy* (experienced by people), or processes or abstractions involving people and their goals (*fragmentation, rift, problem*), whereas in Figure 2 they comprise inanimate entities or processes involving inanimate objects (*signal, alpha Lyman line, changes, convection*). It seems reasonable to conclude that CAUSE implies something undesirable only when human beings, or at least animate beings, are clearly involved. Example 11 in Figure 2 seems to bear this out. In this example animate beings (bees) are involved and perusal of the whole article from which this extract comes indicates that it is the effect on the bee-keepers in Southern Africa that is being considered. Their livelihood is being threatened by the killing of one type of bee by another one, so the destruction of the African bees is undesirable. In this case, then, the evaluative meaning of CAUSE is consistent with the examples in Figure 1. Although it would be wrong to say, therefore, that CAUSE consistently co-occurs with items indicating negative evaluation, it does seem to be the case that when CAUSE co-occurs with an item that involves human self-interest, that is, where evaluation is relevant, that evaluation is very likely to be negative. (See also Section 4 below for a discussion of the correlation of semantic prosody with register.)

This example illustrates that the attitudinal context of a lexical item may be contingent upon other aspects of items in the immediate co-text. In the case of CAUSE this is the nature of the 'thing caused'. In many other cases, the precise phraseology of the lexical item under consideration appears to be the main variable. For example, although *positive influence*, taken in isolation, is about twice as frequent as *negative influence* (120 and 59 instances respectively), the phrase *under the influence of* is typically followed by a noun phrase indicating something undesirable (such as *drugs* or *alcohol*). Even an apparently neutral example, such as *…he believed she was under the influence of her husband,* tends to imply that the husband incited immoral or unlawful behaviour (Hunston 2002:215).

The importance of immediate co-text to the interpretation of a given word is illustrated also by the noun *persistence* and the adjective *persistent*. In context they may indicate either a positive or a negative quality. Numerous instances can be found of the noun being used in contexts which indicate that the quality is one to be approved of, such as: *The Monkey lacks persistence and this can often hamper his progress; [the arrest] is a triumph for persistence; Pupils work with commendable persistence; With great persistence he managed to triumph over [a repressive system].* Yet both the noun and the adjective also occur in contexts where a negative view of 'persistence' is indicated: *...can strike the wrong note with her pushy persistence; persistent offenders; persistent sexism; Con men and charlatans are so thick and so persistent that they make camel drivers at the Pyramids look like Swiss maitres d'.*

Whether 'persistence' in a given instance is interpreted as good or bad seems to depend entirely on the other items in the environment (*managed to triumph over* or *strike the wrong note*). However, the adjective *persistent*, when followed by a noun, co-occurs consistently with items that are evaluatively negative (see Figure 3).

```
1      seats has volunteered despite persistent arm twisting by regional
2      were having to defend against persistent Bradford attacking. In the fir
3  heel of this administration: its persistent determination always to look
4  oard for a grant to rehabilitate persistent drug users, ex-offenders and
5     on thin ice at 4-115 against a persistent England attack. Bevan survived
6         industry, charging it with persistent errors in consumers' details,
7  dentified. <p> Whether it is the persistent intimidation that takes place,
8  ringing in tougher sentences for persistent offenders and ensuring that al
9  of the Ten Hours Bill, which met persistent opposition from government and
10 considerations, thus creating a  persistent paradox. Ainerica's dilemma
11 t unfortunately I can't." After  persistent rain, which reached stair-rod
12    story about one particularly  persistent recruiter. <p> Michael
13    plus the Shamir government's  persistent refusal to give any ground on
14        later this year. Despite  persistent reports of opposition to the
15 th of it. They said there was a  persistent rumour that Mary was actually
16 he practice of folk swayed by a  persistent sense of wonder, chance, and
17 ranssexual an individual with a  persistent sense of discomfort with his o
18 hat this situation is a sign of  persistent sexism, while optimists say th
19 te of the hospital but the most  persistent talk of the more able-bodied
20 e spent on health and pensions. Persistent unemployment is keeping spendi
```

Figure 3.

Clear examples include *drug users, errors, intimidation, offenders, sense of discomfort, sexism* and *unemployment.* Far less clear examples include *recruiter, reports, rumour, sense of wonder* and *talk.* In each case, however, longer co-text confirms the hypothesis that the noun phrase modified by *persistent* indicates something undesirable, at least from the point of view of the producer of the text. The expanded lines in Figure 4 illustrate this.

12 Recruiters also say that if a potential recruit rejects an appeal he or she will be left alone.
  But Michael Hutchinson, an Oakland High School senior, tells a different story about one

*particularly **persistent** recruiter. <p> Michael Hutchinson: He identified himself and told me where he was from, and I said I wasn't interested. And then he went on to say, 'Well, let me tell you a little bit about us first — you know, what we can do for you.'' [The article continues with Hutchinson and his mother expressing dissatisfaction with the behaviour of the (military) recruiter.]*

15 *I talked to a couple of women who had worked with Mary at that clothing factory in Melbourne. … They said there was a **persistent** rumour that Mary was actually a part-time prostitute, specializing in really rough trade.*

16 *Fortune-tellers, magic, witchcraft, spells, and imprecations — even prayer could not alter the course of events, except in the practice of folk swayed by a **persistent** sense of wonder, chance, and evil.*

19 *There are only rumours about the fate of the hospital but the most **persistent** talk of the more able-bodied patients and other people who'd taken refuge in the compound being massacred.*

Figure 4.

However, when *persistent* is used predicatively, the attitudinal implications are less consistent. Although there are examples where what is *persistent* is evaluated negatively, there are others where the opposite is the case, as shown in Figure 5.

Negative attitude
*There are various methods of getting out of a date. You could lie about another boyfriend, say you're not ready to be serious. You could be perpetually tired/overworked/washing your hair. If a man is particularly **persistent** (and the ones you don't want to go out with always are), none of these excuses will deter him.*
*Marrakesh isn't the oldest tourist trap in the Arab world, but it is easily the most aggressive. Con men and charlatans are so thick and so **persistent** that they make camel drivers at the Pyramids look like Swiss maitres d'.*

Positive attitude
*These fights are about the most trivial things, so that the scenes are both funny and sad. … But she is so **persistent**, that Beth that they end up – they have a real break, a very good conversation about religion and about death, they are communicating.*
*Be aware when your body sends you signals that you are doing too much. The signals will be subtle to start with. It is worth paying attention to them, for if you do not, they will become louder and more **persistent**, like a child getting an adult's attention. Illness often comes when the body knows of no other way to you slow down.*

Figure 5.

The outcome of the argument so far, then, is that if a word is observed to co-occur frequently with items with a positive or negative attitudinal meaning that co-occurrence is unlikely to be totally uniform. Statements that a word 'has a semantic prosody', therefore, are likely to be open to substantial criticism unless more precise observations of co-text and phraseology are made.

A second criticism of the concept that a word 'has a (negative or positive) semantic prosody' is that it can involve taking a somewhat simplistic view of attitudinal meaning. Such meaning is often not reducible to a simple 'positive or negative'. It is essentially linked to point of view, so that there is often not one indisputable interpretation of attitude. (As in line 11 of Figure 2 above, *destruction* is a process which is often good for the destroyer but bad for the destroyed.) The adjective *persistent*, for instance, is a word that can be used to indicate a mismatch of viewpoints, with the producer of a text indicating a difference between his or her own values and those of one of the participants in the text. One corpus example comes from a news report describing the theft of a cardboard figure from a video store. The store manager's account of several attempts to steal the figure is reported, culminating in his comment that *There were three young guys out to get him [the figure] and they were very persistent*. From the point of view of the thieves, 'persistence' has enabled them to achieve the goal of obtaining the figure. From the point of view of the manager, 'persistence' has prevented him from achieving his goal of protecting the store's property. This dual viewpoint works because, as has been seen above, the predicative adjective *persistent* can be used to indicate either a desirable or an undesirable quality.

In short, it may be argued that ascribing semantic prosody to a word is over-simplistic. The attitudinal meaning of a word may be altered by its immediate phraseology. The concepts of positive and negative evaluation may themselves be over-simplification, and in any case rest crucially on a notion of point of view.

Writers such as Sinclair, however, use the term 'semantic prosody' in a more subtle way, referring not to simple co-occurrence but to the consistent discourse function of the unit formed by a series of co-occurrences: the 'unit of meaning' (Sinclair 1991:6–9). Looking at the word *budge*, for example (Sinclair 2004:142–147), he notes that it most typically occurs in an extended sequence that includes:

a. A negative, either grammatical or lexical e.g. *I will <u>not</u> budge from my bed; the owner is <u>in no mood to</u> budge on the issue.*
b. An indication of unwillingness e.g. *The Prudential board <u>refused to</u> budge*; or inability e.g. *Firemen…<u>were unable to</u> budge him.*
c. An indication, which may be implied rather than stated, that for one participant in the activity, the lack of movement is a cause of frustration and annoyance e.g.
    a. *<u>Max hurled himself at the door</u>. It did not budge;*
    b. *<u>My ankle is clamped</u> so I can't budge;*
    c. *He knows he must get four vital sequences performed. <u>By day's end he has achieved just two</u>. And still the Lincoln Centre won't budge.*
    d. *To many observers <u>my position seemed cold and hostile</u> but I refused to budge.*

Sinclair's point is that the sequence 'inability + negative + *budge* + (something)' is chosen in contexts where something difficult and important is being attempted, to no avail, and that the sequence 'unwillingness + negative + *budge*' is chosen to express disapproval of someone's lack of flexibility. The sense of frustration is a more complex concept than a simple positive or negative evaluation, and it is clear that it belongs to the sequence as a whole, the unit of meaning, rather than just to the word *budge*.

There are, however, inevitably some counter-examples to the generalisations outlined by Sinclair, and these are instructive in reminding us that the discourse function, or semantic prosody, of expressing difficulty and frustration belongs to the sequence rather than to the word. The first counter-example to be considered is the sequence *did not budge*. As Sinclair (ibid:144) notes, this phrase does often express refusal or inability, though less explicitly than a modal verb would. Examples include: *[They] believed a well-managed chorus of complaints would persuade [name] to step aside... But he did not budge*. When the subject of *budge* is inanimate, however, *did not budge* is not necessarily an instance of the same unit of meaning as *refused to budge*. It may indicate frustration (as in *Max hurled himself at the door. It did not budge*), but it may also indicate a positive achievement, as in the following example:

> He [Otis] chose the New York Exposition to demonstrate his device, standing
> on an open lift high above the ground as his assistant cut the cord supporting it.
> The lift did not budge.

Here the semantic prosody might be described as an expression of surprise on the part of onlookers that something that might be expected to happen (the lift plunges to the ground) has not happened. Other similar examples can be found where the failure of an inanimate object to move is surprising but welcome.

A second apparent counter-example is where the subject of *budge* is *I* or *we*. Unless a clear distinction is made between two points of view (as in *To many observers my position seemed cold and hostile but I refused to budge*, where the emotion surrounding *refused to budge* might be ascribed to the observers rather than to the speaker), sequences such as *I refused to budge* or *we will not budge* cannot have the same semantic prosody as *he refused to budge*. Instead we find that these sequences consistently express an attitude of determination in the face of opposition rather than frustration. Examples include: *It was like the Middle East peace process, drawing up the areas where compromise was possible and those where I refused to budge*; *The Prime Minister rejected resounding calls for the resignation of the government. 'I will not budge,' he said*; *He tried to persuade me, but I wouldn't budge*.

In other words, an examination of the word *budge* in a corpus leads to not one but two observations. One is that the (overwhelmingly) most frequent phraseology around the word involves a negative, an indication of unwillingness or inability, and a subject that is other than a first person pronoun. The second is that where that phraseology is found, the discourse function of the sequence is to express frustration in the face of difficulty. If the phraseology changes, the semantic prosody is also different. This is not particularly surprising, but it serves as a useful reminder that, in Sinclair's examples at least, semantic prosody is a discourse function of a sequence rather than a property of a word.

3.   Semantic prosody: observation, explanation or prediction?

The second issue to be taken up in this paper is the more general one about whether phenomena that reflect frequency of occurrence, including but not restricted to semantic prosody, have an observational, an explanatory or a predictive value. At issue here is the relationship between a corpus of many instances of language, a single instance of language, and the reader/hearer.

Any identification of a recurring pattern rests on **observation**. It may be observed, for example, that a sequence of elements has a fairly consistent discourse function. To take another example from Sinclair (2004:35–36; 2003), the phrase *true feelings* typically occurs in a sequence such as *he may not want to admit his true feelings...*, which expresses a 'reluctance or inability' to talk about emotional matters (Sinclair 2004:35). Observations such as these are important where information about lexical items is being given, such as in dictionary definitions. In Sinclair's terms, a good definition should give information about the unit of meaning, rather than just the headword, and should where possible indicate the discourse function of that unit. (In practice this can require considerable skill to do. The *Collins COBUILD Advanced Learners Dictionary* (2003), which is unfortunately silent on the subject of *true feelings*, does define *budge* in terms of the meaning of the whole unit: 'If someone will not budge on a matter... they refuse to change their mind or to come to an agreement', but not in terms of its function. Such a definition might begin: 'If you wish to indicate that you are frustrated that someone refuses to change their mind...', but it quickly becomes unwieldy.)

Many writers, however, use observations of recurrent patterning as a way of **explaining** subjective reactions to individual instances of language. At its least interesting, this can be used to explain why the speech or writing of non-native speakers of English can sometimes be misleading or sound amusing to native speakers (e.g. Hunston 2002:60–62, 214–216). (The investigation of *persistent* reported above, for example, was inspired by the sentence in a student's dissertation: *I would like to thank my supervisor for his persistent help and advice.*) Where unusual collocations occur in native speaker discourse, the addressee may draw what might be called a 'collocational inference'. For example, an email to a colleague contains the clause *Thank you for your characteristically helpful [message]*. The recipient of the email feels oddly slighted, even though his/her message has been described as 'helpful'. A check on the Bank of English corpus reveals that whereas *characteristically helpful* is rare (it does not occur at all in the current BoE), *characteristically unhelpful* is a little more frequent (3 occurrences). Grice (1975) might comment that the Maxim of Manner appears to have been flouted, in that a less-frequent collocation has been used instead of a more-frequent and morphologically related one. Whereas Grice might talk in terms of implicature (the message implicates 'you are being unhelpful, and typically so'), the term 'collocational inference' stresses that what is at issue here is the interpretation of the addressee rather than the intention of the addressor. Identification of the oddness of the collocation serves to explain the inference drawn. (The writer of the email, of course, might argue strenuously that no such implication was intended.)

Aside from such minor cases, observation of what is frequent can be used in the service of explanation of rhetorical or stylistic effect. Perhaps most famously, Louw (1993, 1997) compares extracts from individual literary texts with a general corpus in order to account for aesthetic response to the text. He suggests that words and phrases in the target text carry a resonance from their use in other texts which adds to the complexity of meaning in the target text. One of the most compelling examples is that of the lines from the Yeats poem *Memory* (which expresses the effects of first love on subsequent relationships): *One had a lovely face/And two or three had charm/But charm and face were in vain/Because the mountain grass/ Cannot but keep the form/Where the mountain hare has lain*. Louw (1997) reports that (only) one of his students saw an anti-female bias in the line *but charm and face were in vain*, but had difficulty in supporting her reaction with any evidence. Investigation of a corpus showed that a frequent use of *in vain* is in co-occurrence with indications of goal-oriented activity: *Giovanni sought in vain a means of retreat; the captains tried in vain to maintain some semblance of order; I had waited in vain*. In using *in vain*, Louw and his student argue, the poem implies that the women are manipulative, unspontaneous, and this implication in turn can be interpreted as representing a bias against women. This is a remarkably subtle reading of a brief phrase. Like all readings of literary works, it is subjective and resistant to 'proof', but at least a warrant has been given for the student's personal reading of the poem.

Such exploitation of intertextuality, as with all creativity (cf. Carter 2004), is not restricted to literary texts. For example, Hunston (1995) has argued that intertextuality can be used to construe layers of points of view in a text via attribution.

In the examples given, a person or group is construed as holding a point of view from which the writer of the text is distanced. Only one instance will be repeated here. It involves the verb *acknowledge*, which typically construes agreement by a speaker with a proposition which runs counter to their more general point of view, as in *even investors... acknowledge that the unions are key* (investors do not usually hold unions in high esteem but do so in this instance). Where the reported speaker is an opponent of the writer, the semantic prosody might be described as a kind of triumph that the attributee has been forced to concede a point against him or herself. The example discussed by Hunston comes from a review of a book by the historian Ellis which comments, apparently approvingly, that *Ellis is perhaps the first white social historian to acknowledge that without the machine gun, Africa may never have been enslaved.* It is argued that this construes Ellis as taking a pro-African view in this case although in general, like other white social historians, being opposed to that view. That meaning is not observable from the example in isolation but from the implications of the verb *acknowledge*, observed intertextually.

What all these examples have in common is the use of observation of recurrence or typicality in a large corpus of texts to explain a subjective reaction to an individual text. They belong to a more general tradition of calling on the discontinuity between the norm and the individual example to account for the recognition of a variety of stylistic effects. If the reaction is acknowledged to be entirely subjective, the use of a corpus to account for it is relatively uncontentious. For example, if I claim to be amused by a student thanking his supervisor for *his persistent help and advice*, and use corpus evidence to explain why I personally think this is funny, few would find this interesting enough to be objectionable. If, on the other hand, I argue that all readers are or should be amused by the student's words, on the grounds that it does not accord with typical usage, the argument is more open to attack. This is what might be called the predictive value of frequent occurrence, and it is to this that we now turn.

The **predictive** line of argument, articulated explicitly by Louw (1993), suggests that if a word or sequence is used in an unusual way, this necessarily implies irony or insincerity. This is a much stronger claim than the explanatory one, with much more at stake. As a result, it is at the same time more open to attack (e.g. Whitsitt 2005) and potentially more useful. On the positive side, it lessens the subjectivity involved in the explanatory view of semantic prosody. It accounts for consensual reactions to texts as well as for individual ones. On the other hand, it assumes a uniformity of meaning, an intolerance of individual usage, that many find unacceptable. As an example, I shall reconsider the example *to the point of*. I have argued that *to the point of* is used to link a less saturated evaluative item with a more saturated one[3] (as in *thin* to the point of *emaciation*) and, moreover, that the evaluation is always negative (Hunston 2004:163–165). Figure 6 shows some examples.

```
wood' (VSB 168) - and abundant to the point of extravagance (VSB 167). Withi
   s supposed to be puritanical to the point of ingenuousness, is obviously v
   Rushdie, for one). Convoluted to the point of dislocation - there are stori
   Willie's subjects are laconic to the point of silence; there are interviews
      in these years was hermetic to the point of solipsism — a stance of icy
         labourer and sus-picious to the point of paranoia. <p> By extraordinar
      to its old self, precious to the point of self-parody, a magnet for
professional manner was strict to the point of severity. She brought crystal
   and with back play ponderous to the point of stationary, it was a wonder t
organisation, and we are naive to the point of idiocy… <subh> Naughtie
```

Figure 6.

Most apparent counter-examples can be shown not to be so: even if the word following *to the point of* is one that is often used positively, it can be shown with more co-text that in the environment of *to the point of* it is used negatively. Here are two examples:

> *This assessment, given by one of the nine members of his committee, reflects a genuine warmth and respect for their chairman. Unfailingly courteous, **to the point of** gentleness, Lord Nolan also displayed a fierce independence and skill in both bringing together his disparate committee members, some Conservative, like the former defence secretary Tom King, some deeply embedded in the much criticised parliamentary system...*

> *Altnaharrie isn't perfect. There is too much cream in some dishes, and others — my pigeon for example — were so multi-layered as almost to cancel themselves out. The tone of the place can sometimes feel hushed **to the point of** being reverential, as if the ferry journey was a prelude to entering a Temple of Gastronomy. Clearly this is highly artistic food and, as Gunn says, 'the meal has to balance. On the palette and in the stomach you should feel comfortable but also excited...*

Although *gentleness* and *reverential* are not in isolation clear indications of something undesirable, the expanded context shows that, in these instances, the qualities of gentleness and reverence are not viewed positively. So far, then, the argument bears out Louw's point; a writer using *to the point of* necessarily implies a negative evaluation and this overrides the usual meaning of other words in the immediate environment of the phrase. The evidence is not one hundred per cent consistent, however. I have found one example (and this is unlikely to be completely unique) where *to the point of* is followed by an adjective that is used entirely positively:

> *At 23 and with just one exhibition behind her, Brisbane painter Hazel Dooney is fresh **to the point of** invigoration. Her bold and colourful paintings combine elements of youth culture into pop art which is appealing not only for its pure aesthetics but also for its contemporary nature.*

Following Louw, we might deduce that the writer is being ironic or insincere, and we might expect there to be evidence somewhere in the text as a whole that this is the case. Having read the whole article, I can say that this is not so. It is possible, of course, that the writer harbours a secret grudge against Dooney, unwittingly revealed by his or her choice of phrasing, but there is no textual evidence for this interpretation. It seems, then, that this is simply an atypical use of the phrase *to the point of.*

This rare counter-example poses few problems for the observational and explanatory use of the concept of semantic prosody. The observation that *to the point of* usually and typically occurs with negative evaluation still holds. A language learner could be given this information without fear of contradiction. In addition, a reader who considers the cited sentence about Dooney to be somewhat humorous has plenty of evidence to account for their reaction. It is only if we argue that this writer must necessarily be lying, or joking, or that every reader will make that assumption, that we run into trouble.

4.   Attitudinal meaning and register-specific corpora

One of the arguments sometimes made with respect to semantic prosody and other aspects of attitudinal meaning is that it is register-specific.[4] With respect to CAUSE, for example, it would be possible to suggest that this verb loses its association with negative evaluation when it occurs in 'scientific' registers. A more sustainable argument, however, might be that, as pointed out above, the attitudinal meaning associated with CAUSE applies only when the 'caused entity' concerns animate beings, their activities and goals. Where the 'caused entity' is an inanimate object unrelated to human goals no attitudinal meaning is implied. If a register makes more use of the second phenomenon than the first, it will appear that in that register CAUSE has no attitudinal meaning. In other words, rather than suggesting that register can make attitudinal meaning appear or disappear we might argue that particular registers select one lexical phenomenon more frequently than another. This would be in keeping with Halliday's view of register as comprising the outcome of a set of selections from a more general language system (Halliday & Matthiessen 2004:27–28).

Other aspects of attitudinal meaning in specific registers might be illustrat-ed using a very small corpus of 13 articles from the journal *Applied Linguistics*, each of which takes an overtly antagonistic attitude towards another researcher or group of researchers.[5] One noticeable feature of this 'conflict corpus' is that, for very many words in it, a set of concordance lines will demonstrate negative evalu-ation. The corpus-user might be tempted in each case to attribute this evaluation to the word or phrase under investigation. This is the case in any corpus which con-sists exclusively of texts whose purpose is to evaluate or to exert overt persuasion.

There are, however, at least three different phenomena at work in the conflict corpus and it is important that they are distinguished from each other. Firstly, some phrases in the conflict corpus do appear to imply a negative evaluation. For example, my intuition is that the phrase *seem(s) to think*, used to report the views of another writer, suggests a scornful attitude on the part of the reporter, as in *Where are his arguments? He **seems to think** that he is under no obligation to pro-vide any. He makes his ex cathedra pronouncement and that's that* (Hunston 2005). It is difficult, however, to distinguish the effect imparted by the phrase *seems to think* from the general negative evaluation surrounding it. Investigation of both a larger corpus of research articles in the field of Applied Linguistics and of a ref-erence corpus, however, suggest that *seems to think* (or more generally SEEM *to* followed by a verb of attribution) is indeed used mostly in contexts where the reporter not only disagrees with the reported writer but attributes to him or her a lack of common sense as in this example from a corpus of spoken English:

Speaker 1:   *He **seems to think** it's cool to do this*
Speaker 2:   *Yeah I know it's bloody stupid isn't it it's really*
Speaker 1:   *And it's not cool*
Speaker 2:   *No it's not it's bloody unprofessional and stupid*

It is also the case that whereas in the conflict corpus *seem(s) to think* accounts for a relatively large proportion of the total instances of *think* (about 20%), in the general corpus the equivalent proportion is less than 1%. In other words, the se-quence *seem(s) to think* can be demonstrated to co-occur with a particular type of judgement in a variety of contexts, but to occur in the conflict corpus relatively more frequently than in other collections of texts. We can be confident that in this case the phrase in question does contribute to the attitudinal meaning in the texts in the corpus.

Secondly, however, some words co-occur with negative evaluation because they are the focus of the dispute being enacted. In a sub-set of articles discussing corpus linguistics and language teaching, *significance* is one such word. Negative evaluations of *significance* are common, as in the examples shown in Figure 7.

1   *the **significance** of this is limited;*
2   *of considerable **significance** only if they allow their limitations;*
3   *a problem [relating to] the extent to which **significance** can be assigned;*
4   *unwarranted discourse **significance**;*
5   *it is problematic to assign discourse **significance**;*
6   *[it is wrong to] assign keyword **significance**…without reference to a norm;*
7   *frequency is not necessarily the same as interpretative **significance***

Figure 7.

At first glance it may appear that *significance* has negative attitudinal meaning in this corpus, but it would be more true to say that it can be observed to be a site or an attractor of evaluation.

Finally, it must be recognised that some words or phrases co-occur with negative evaluation simply because there is a lot of negative evaluation in the texts concerned. For example, 20 out of the 28 instances of *to have* in the conflict corpus have indications of negative attitude within a short co-text. The sentences themselves are varied — Figure 8 shows some examples.

1   *Since little L2 acquisition, let alone 'naturalistic' L2 acquisition appears **to have** been involved in the experiment, it is difficult to see how the findings bear upon the CPH in any direct manner. A more convincing study…*
2   *It is simply not possible for mental representations to become less analysed. To claim that it is possible is either **to have** a radically different interpretation of representation or to assign fundamental responsibility in learning to forgetting. [Name]'s error is to confuse…*
3   *The absurdity of [Name]'s blackboxing claim seems even **to have** dawned on [Name] at one point*
4   *However, as I hope to demonstrate in a moment, if we dig under the surface a little, we very quickly find reason **to have** doubts about the solid foundation which [Name] wishes to attribute to SLA.*
5   *Secondly, this misunderstanding of my text seems **to have** primed [Name] to misunderstand [Name]'s text as well.*

Figure 8.

The point is that in a corpus of this kind, a concordance of almost any word will give similar results and it would be misleading to assign any kind of significance to the presence of evaluation surrounding *to have*.

In short, it would be true to say that in this specific corpus the items such as *significance* and *to have* frequently co-occur with negative evaluation. It would be a mistake, however, to account for this in terms of attitudinal meaning associated with those items, let alone semantic prosody. In neither case does the item in question add to the evaluative meaning of the texts.

5. Conclusion

This paper has attempted to discuss two issues. The first is the applicability of the term 'semantic prosody' to at least two different phenomena: the discourse function of an extended unit of meaning, and the attitudinal meanings typically associated with a word or phrase. The second is the more general issue of how corpus evidence is to be interpreted: the relationship between the typical and the atypical, and the extent to which corpus evidence of what is typical can be used to predict, rather than simply explain, the impact of an individual instance.

In relation to the first issue, my own suggestion would be that the term 'semantic prosody' is best restricted to Sinclair's use of it to refer to the discourse function of a unit of meaning, something that is resistant to precise articulation and that may well not be definable as simply 'positive' or 'negative'. I would suggest that a different term, such as 'semantic preference' or perhaps 'attitudinal preference', is used to refer to the frequent co-occurrence of a lexical item with items expressing a particular evaluative meaning. On the other hand, as 'prosody' and 'preference' are both metaphors, more transparent terminology in both cases might be less open to confusion.

In relation to the second issue, and in general to the 'transfer' of attitudinal meaning from one context to another, there seems to me to be a genuine dilemma. On the one hand, there is a strong argument that meaning does not exist except in context (Teubert 2003). It seems illogical to say, therefore, that a word or phrase can carry its meaning across from one context to another (and Whitsitt (2005) offers further arguments in support of this view). This absolves us from the need to find reasons for non-attitudinal uses of CAUSE or to agonise over rare counter-examples such as *fresh to the point of invigoration*. All we need to say is that CAUSE often occurs in the context of undesirable situations, but not always, and that *to the point of* is usually followed by a noun phrase indicating something undesirable, but not always.

On the other hand, while meaning may not be transferable from one text to another, resonances of intertextuality are difficult to deny. They allow us to interpret *cause a fire* differently from *light a fire*, to understand that *courteous to the point of gentleness* strikes a cautionary note about the quality of gentleness and to perceive that *seems to think* is not simply a hedged variant of *thinks*.

The dilemma, then, is that the notion of 'transferring' attitudinal meaning from the majority of instances to a single instance sometimes works very well in explaining interpretations of that single instance. In other cases it is irrelevant. To say that a word cannot possibly carry an attitudinal meaning from one context to another is to deny an explanation of much implied meaning. On the other hand, to argue that this necessarily happens always, just because it clearly often happens, is equally misleading.

Finally, this paper has argued for care in interpreting the attitudinal meaning encountered in citations from corpora. Typical evaluative meaning has been shown to be associated with precise details of phraseology. It has been suggested that the identification of attitudinal meaning in a set of concordance lines is insufficient in itself to allow conclusions to be drawn about the meaning of the node of those lines. It has been argued also that treating evaluative meaning as a simple distinction between 'good' and 'bad' can be over-simplistic.

This paper was written, as were all the papers in this collection, in the expectation that John Sinclair would have the opportunity to respond to it and to engage in a debate around it. His untimely death prevented that. The paper reflects my sense of having failed always to appreciate the subtlety of John's arguments. John saw an early draft of the paper, corrected a couple of factual errors and said he was looking forward to discussing the issues raised in it. Unfortunately we were never able to have that discussion.

Notes

1. Except where otherwise stated, corpus examples concordance lines and calculations of frequency in this paper come from the Bank of English (BoE) corpus.

2. I am grateful to Prof Wolfgang Teubert and Dr Peter White for making this point with respect to CAUSE.

3. I have taken the term 'saturated' from Appraisal theory (developed by Jim Martin and Peter White).

4. This is not an argument made by Sinclair, however, whose work is based on general, reference corpora.

5. I am grateful to the publishers of *Applied Linguistics* for giving permission to collect the corpus, and to Nicholas Groom for assistance in compiling the corpus.

References

Carter, R. (2004). *Language and Creativity: the Art of Common Talk*. London: Routledge.
Collins COBUILD Advanced Learner's English Dictionary. (2003). Glasgow: HarperCollins.
Grice, H. P. (1975). Logic and conversation. In P. Cole & J. Morgan (Eds.), *Syntax and Semantics* Vol. 3. *Speech Acts*. (pp. 41–58). New York: Academic Press.

Halliday, M. A. K. & Matthiessen, C. (2004). *An Introduction to Functional Grammar* (Third Edition). London: Arnold.

Hunston, S. (2005). Conflict and consensus: construing opposition in Applied Linguistics. In E. Tognini-Bonelli & G. del Lungo Camiciotti (Eds.), *Strategies in Academic Discourse* (pp. 1–16). Amsterdam: Benjamins.

Hunston, S. (2004). Counting the uncountable: problems of identifying evaluation in a text and in a corpus. In A. Partington, J. Morley & L. Haarman (Eds.), *Corpora and Discourse* (pp. 157–188). Bern: Peter Lang.

Hunston, S. (2002). *Corpora in Applied Linguistics.* Cambridge: Cambridge University Press.

Hunston, S. (1995). A corpus study of some English verbs of attribution. *Functions of Language* 2, 133–158.

Louw, B. (1997). The role of corpora in critical literary appreciation. In A. Wichmann, S. Fligelstone, T. McEnery & G. Knowles (Eds.), *Teaching and Language Corpora* (pp. 240–251). London: Longman.

Louw, B. (1993). Irony in the text or insincerity in the writer? — the diagnostic potential of semantic prosodies. In M. Baker, G. Francis & E. Tognini-Bonelli (Eds.), *Text and Technology: in honour of John Sinclair* (pp. 157–176). Amsterdam: Benjamins.

Martin, J. R. & White, P. R. R. (2005). *The Language of Evaluation: Appraisal in English.* London: Palgrave Macmillan.

Partington, A. (2004). "Utterly content in each other's company": semantic prosody and semantic preference. *International Journal of Corpus Linguistics* 9(1), 131–156.

Partington, A. (1998). *Patterns and Meanings.* Amsterdam: Benjamins.

Sinclair, J. M. (2004). *Trust the Text: Language, Corpus and Discourse.* London: Routledge.

Sinclair, J. M. (2003). *Reading Concordances: an Introduction.* London: Longman.

Sinclair J. M. (1991). *Corpus, Concordance, Collocation.* Oxford: Oxford University Press.

Stubbs, M. (2001). *Words and Phrases: Corpus Studies of Lexical Semantics.* New York: Blackwell.

Stubbs, M. (1996). *Text and Corpus Analysis.* Oxford: Blackwell.

Stubbs, M. (1995). Collocations and semantic profiles: on the cause of the trouble with quantitative studies. *Functions of Language* 2, 1–33.

Teubert, W. (2003). Writing, hermeneutics, and corpus linguistics. *Logos and Language* 2, 1–17.

Tognini-Bonelli, E. (2001). *Corpus Linguistics at Work.* Amsterdam: Benjamins.

Whitsitt, S. (2005). A critique of the concept of semantic prosody. *International Journal of Corpus Linguistics* 10(3), 283–305.

Trust and text, text as trust

Michael Toolan
University of Birmingham

In this essay I celebrate and interrogate John Sinclair's seminal paper, 'Trust the text', a paper in which several radically new ideas about the role of prospection and encapsulation in the reader's processing of text are outlined. I mention some of the ways in which trust is fundamental to matters of language and cooperative communication, but also try to enlarge on what I think Sinclair has in mind. In reading on (and not re-reading), as we nearly always do when confronted with text, we are trusting the text in a more particular way, trusting it to have been composed in such a way that what follows will answer or complete what has gone before. This text-trust is perhaps the most fundamental structuring principle in written discourse, and mostly we apply it unwittingly; Sinclair's paper broaches some lines of enquiry by which linguists might develop a fuller explanation of it.

Keywords: prospection, encapsulation, temporality, textual progression

1. Preliminaries

A text is an act of trust, a process of entrusting, whether we like it or not. Leaving a note on the fridge, prefaced *This is just to say*, telling your partner that you've eaten the plums (*they were delicious // so sweet // and so cold*) as William Carlos Williams did, is bad news if you are that plum-centred partner, but what levels of entrusting are involved. How absurd, for example, if on opening the fridge door the partner finds the plums inside untouched, topped by a little note saying *just kidding* (see Haiman (1998) on this common conversational gambit). No-one, no-one prospects that scenario. No, we trust that speaker A has honestly (relevantly, in an orderly and sufficiently informative manner, Gricewise) represented to addressee B what they have done. And all prefaced by the suitably self-conscious *this is just to say*: where no saying is involved, no speaking is possible, we trust that in the writing a kind of saying is performed. And 'just', as if the power of our disciplined markings on a surface to count as a responsible saying, averring (to use Sinclair's term), undertaking, promising, confessing, or other self-declaring, were a small thing! Similarly on the UK banknotes in my pocket one Merlyn Lowther, Chief Cashier, writing on behalf of the Bank of England, "promises to pay the bearer on demand the sum of TWENTY Pounds". And I trust him. Merlyn Lowther, what sort of chap is called Merlyn Lowther, you wonder, and have you read the faint signature correctly? So (in July 2005) I google the name and find not only that Merlyn Lowther was no chap at all, but the first woman chief cashier of the Bank of England. Also, and more alarmingly, that she retired in December 2003! Where is Ms Lowther now, and is her promise still valid? Who knows? Yet I do not panic: I trust the text.

Where does the phrase *trust the text* come from? I mean other than from Sinclair himself? I had imagined — and think I still do — that he partly had in mind the memorable slogan of D. H. Lawrence: "Never trust the teller, trust the tale". But trusting the text isn't quite the same as trusting the tale, perhaps. In addition Sinclair may have intended a swipe at the deconstructionist and postmodernist *dis*trust of the text, which was all the rage at the end of the 1980's when his thinking on the topic of this paper must have been evolving.

I also did a google search of the phrase *trust the text*. I was amused to find that my own talk on Sinclair's paper, at an English department seminar in 2004, popped up as the fourth result, of about 1500. The first two results were to Sinclair's book; and the third, which he might also have liked, was to a Burns Night supper. A further result was a list of prescriptions as to how to teach and preach Calvinism:

> Trust the text and the people will trust you to be faithful to the text.

(This injunction should be enunciated in a 'Scottish-Calvinist' accent, of course, if we are to be consistent with Firth's ideas about accent and meaning, when he suggested that it is part of the meaning of being American to sound like one). There are in fact numerous biblical or theological uses of the phrase among those 1500 Google hits, along with quite a few pertaining to theatrical performance and what the dramaturgy should be rooted in. Then there are some like the following, from an Oxford University web page for a course on James Joyce:

> Under no circumstances should you trust the text of the edition entitled *Ulysses: A Reader's Edition*, edited by Danis Rose, to be Joyce's text.

So just to sum up, I take it that Sinclair does have in mind a contrast between linguists and texts, especially the over-confident linguist who might approach the text with too many fixed assumptions about what they will find there. He wants us to give texts a fresh, trusting look. In what follows I will work through what I see as major points in the 'Trust the Text' paper; if this sometimes seems too much like mere paraphrase of the paper itself, I would justify this by arguing that the paper's claims were radical enough — and sometimes opaque enough! — to warrant such an attempt to re-state them in a partly different way, in the hope that this might help me, and others, better to understand those claims.

2.   The implications of 'inadequate evidence'

Sinclair begins with a sentence authored by Randolph Quirk, writing in *The European* newspaper:

> *The implications are daunting.*

He tells us that he will recurringly allude to this sentence's 'discourse function'. But almost immediately he turns to some general and prefatory observations about how linguistics has tended to be based on too little evidence, degenerate data, causing too much reliance on speculation, rather than fact. The idea of 'too little evidence' is an odd claim — but then part of Sinclair's impact (like that of other recent British grammarians and linguists) has derived from the oddity of some of his claims. But it is still odd to say that linguists have had too little evidence to go on. Not merely because they and we are bombarded with language all of our waking lives, but also because it is hard to imagine an adherent of any established discipline or science using quite that formulation: would a geologist say there was, until recently, too little evidence for us to do useful geology? Or an epidemiologist, or a medical scientist, or even a social scientist? With what contexts of situation is the phrase *too little evidence* associated? Perhaps chiefly historical investigations or those that reach back towards pre-history, and abandoned or unsuccessful criminal prosecutions — where, as Sinclair might well point out, the proportion of speculation to fact is unacceptably high.

But I think it significant that Sinclair laments there has been too little evidence, and not too little information, or even too little data. He knows that what we call evidence is a particular marshalling or construal of information, a marshalling of it for particular purposes. So what he means by (to paraphrase) "too little evidence for good factual linguistics" is perhaps something like 'insufficient opportunity to cast and present the information in the way needed to substantiate, and render acceptable as more than speculations, the descriptions of lexical and multi-word behaviour and patterning that I regard as of central interest and importance'. In short, we can hardly claim that linguists in the past had 'too little language' on which to work; rather it is a question of claiming that, in the past, there was not available (or, if available, neglected) sufficient language that was gathered, recorded, transcribed, brought together in some form that permitted certain kinds of scrutiny and analy-sis (especially, analyses based in reading). Or to put things very specifically, we did not have, in the past, easy access to and inspectability of the kinds of evidence that facilitate the identification of collocations, multi-word prosodies, and similar statements about quasi-idiomatic lexical patterning. But the evidence was always there, and if one had had enough harmless drudges to help one pore over texts, record and count instances…. By the same token there was in the past sufficient material to enable (indeed, to make seem natural) other kinds of linguistic analysis (of a non-collocation-oriented variety), for good or ill, including the writing of grammars and dictionaries. The most crucial enabling condition was the existence of writing, the emergence of which transformed humankind's ways of conceiving of language.

Incidentally it is possible to see certain similarities between the very idea of trust and that of collocation. Collocation has been said to denote the lexical or phrasal company that particular words keep. Or, if we want to move away from the *phrasal* 'head + complements' emphasis that focus on node and collocates fosters, collocation is the marked tendency of words to co-occur in patterns or structures where, by virtue of the frequency of the association, part of the meaning of the pattern is distributed like a prosody across the entirety of the pattern and cannot be assigned exclusively to one or another of the component words (like opaque idioms, the pattern resists semantic decomposition). It is true that there is often asymmetry in collocational relations, which may well cause a rarely-used word A to collocate in a large proportion of its occurrences with a frequently-used word B, while B's 'predictive' bond with A is much weaker: B is far more phrasally sig-nificant to A than A is to B. Nevertheless, there is always some degree of interde-pendence and reciprocity involved. So too, is there in trust — even where the trust tends to be transitive chiefly in one direction. That is, trust breaks down, does not truly exist, where the person or thing trusted turns out not to be trustworthy. It is not enough for the initiating party to be trusting, if that trust is not returned. So in trust as in collocation there is an interesting degree of bi-directionality of the process involved.

But stepping away from the phrasal vs collocational grammar opposition, it might be noted that for certain kinds of study, arguably, we still have far too little **objectified** evidence on which to work, even with the massive written corpora at our disposal: studies of eye-movements and gaze shifts during interaction, for ex-ample. The Bank of English's half an American billion written/transcribed words can certainly grow larger, in all kinds of comparative ways. But if spoken English also turns out to look differently when we can look at a lot of it electronically and digitally, then we do not yet have the resources to confirm this. So we can surely predict that the nearer future of English studies should bring a corpus of record-ings of spoken English. The digitised recording of course is not the hard bit, the accessibility and manipulation issues are. That is, a young female Japanese learner of English wants to know how to order a coffee and croissant at a Manchester café, and then wants to hear recordings of real instances of, say, young women saying "I'd like a double tall Americano with room for milk and a ham croissant please, to eat in". And so on for thousands of similar slices of real spoken English. Well, for thousands first, then very soon for tens of thousands. How far off is this? I expect to learn that Sony or CUP or the Chinese are already at work on this, but if they are not, they soon will be. The multilingual corpus tools and voice-recognition software is already in place.

And then after the oral/aural corpus linguistic generation of databanks and software and research, there should emerge audio-visual corpora, again of massive extent and scope, and again with exponentially more difficult problems of access, retrieval, manipulation, and comparison and clustering of instances, than were the case in the earlier text and speech corpora. A crucial question must be what impact such developments might have on corpus linguistics. Might it prompt the promo-tion of segmenting language for analysis, on neither traditional grammatical nor lexical-phraseological bases? E.g., turn by turn segmentation of the language? Or breath intake by breath intake? Or from one gaze-shift by a speaker to their next gaze-shift? I certainly think we may (gradually, resistingly) move away from work-ing only with units and rules that are deeply exploitative of our favourite mode, writing.

3.   False projections and model-building

Sinclair's paper emphasizes the radical shift in how we can look at language that has been enabled by both audio-recording equipment and, more recently, com-puter technology: these have brought quantitative and qualitative changes, he says, where we need to be guarded about 'projecting' techniques of analysis from one language area to others. Two points in particular are stressed: the need for open-ness to new techniques of description and analysis; and the need for open-ness about re-thinking our theoretical assumptions, leading to a perhaps quite radi-cally new theory of language or discourse. Seemingly intended as demonstrations of how borrowing and projecting old models and techniques can end up being a mistake, even a disastrous mistake, Sinclair cites two examples: the work of Zellig Harris in the early 1950s, and his 'distributionalist' discourse analysis. He suggests

[This] led Harris to the idea that stretches of language which, though physically different, were systematically related, could be regarded as essentially the same. This was articulated as grammatical transformation. It is an object lesson in what can go wrong if you project your techniques upwards into other areas without careful monitoring and adaptation.

(Sinclair 2004:11)

Sinclair notes that Harris in turn led to Chomsky, which brought cognitive, non-textual linguistics into the world, and all our woe. But I would be interested to know precisely where he judges that Harris's 'going wrong' began (it is not explained within the paper). Perhaps it lay in the conceptualising of related syntagms as 'grammatical transformations' rather than as semantic transforms or discourse partners. (On the other hand, at least the citing of Zellig Harris's work at this point is properly motivated and explained. Interestingly, at about this same time of writing — the early 1990's — Harris is being discussed in a rather more combative and polemical paper by Widdowson, in which he takes CDA and the work of Fairclough (1992) to task; but in the Widdowson paper (1995) the motivation for mentioning Harris is much less clear. For both Sinclair and Widdowson, Harris's work seems to serve as best exemplar of how discourse analysis of an earlier generation was instructively wrongheaded.)

In any event, Sinclair's second example of faulty projection of an old model is his own work using a scale and category model, and presumably one including acts, moves, exchanges and transactions, on the structure of spoken interaction: "I cheerfully admit 'mea culpa' here", he writes (Sinclair 2004:11). But he goes on to point out that the model has been serviceable and is still developing. So quite what was wrong with it, again, we are never explicitly told.

Turning again to how he thinks things **ought** to be done, particularly in relation to discourse, Sinclair emphasizes the need for a model of discourse which is special to discourse: "we should build a model which emphasizes the distinctive features of discourse. A special model for discourse will offer an explanation of those features of discourse that are unique to it, or characteristic... or prominent..." (ibid.:12). And to do this we now have the considerable assistance of computers. But computers, he stresses, will only tell us more reliably what we already suppose or predict (a kind of "checking on detail" (ibid.:12)) — so it is particularly important now to re-visit our suppositions and predictions, and see whether radically new ones should be pursued. He proceeds to offer one of these radically new suppositions or hypotheses, which he describes as stronger than the usual ones encountered, and "explicit enough to identify a large number of cases automatically". It relates to the prospective features of spoken discourse: "For me the study of discourse began in earnest when I classified initiations in exchanges according to how they preclassify what follows" (ibid.:12).

It is at roughly this point that what Sinclair has to say bears directly on my own interests in studying narrative progression in fictional texts, especially short stories. My interest is in the reader's expectations — their prescience if you like — and how these are shaped by and in the course of the progression of a literary text. And I have also become interested in whether and how corpus linguistic analyses can assist us in understanding how text-progression guides expectation. Can corpus analysis assist us in understanding literary texts not merely as products, but also as processes: the process of writing a text and the process of reading one?

Expectation relates directly to those two classic questions of discourse and conversational analytical theory: 'Why this now?' 'What next?' It bears, also, on questions of collocatability and idiomaticity. It is surely also closely linked to what Sinclair calls the prospective features of discourse: a reader develops expectations on the basis of what the text prospects. And as he remarks: "The more that attention has been focussed on the prospective qualities of discourse the more accurate and powerful the description has become" (Sinclair 2004:13).

As I have already noted, Sinclair suggests that we should build a 'special model' for discourse. But as we attempt to do so, we must address a characteristic of those discourses called novels and short stories, which sets them apart from the teacher-pupil exchange, or the service encounter, or the academic article, or the casual conversation, or many other kinds of discourse, by virtue of their asserted completeness and autonomy (which is also to say their partial escape from genre-boundedness). A short story or novel is something that purports to be, and is apprehended as, 'all there is', therefore complete in texture and structure and wording, to a degree that seems unmatched by most other language uses, and particularly most other non-literary uses. This makes the language of a story or novel somewhat different from other kinds of language — at least it does in western literary cultures where we require literature to be innovative and distinctive. In particular the language of a story isn't fairly thought of as a sample from a larger body with common generic or registral features. We cannot, as readers or linguists, assume that one novel (or sonnet) is doing broadly the same job as another novel, with the same phrases and using the same registral features, but with 'variation' in content or wording. By contrast a particular stretch of language on the bus, or in the newspaper, or during a service-encounter, or between professional and client, is justifiably seen, in one light, as a sample of a larger body of language activity of the same kind. In one sense, yes, a story by Alice Munro (the renowned contemporary Canadian short story writer) is just another use of English, just another piece of discourse, in tacit communion with all other samples of English, just as a lawyer's letter or a travel article is.

On the other hand a Munro story is sufficiently unique that it comprises just the words she chose in just the order she chose, and no others, the whole being subject to copyright in ways only infrequently applicable to other kinds of language use (or, its particularity outweighing its generic qualities, by contrast with most non-literary texts where the reverse is usually true). These issues are too complex and contentious to be covered here, and my emphasizing the uniqueness and completeness of the individual story will be countered by reference to such story collections as 'Dubliners', 'Winesburg', 'Ohio', and so on. But we do not, in the act of reading, treat any of the stories within those collections **as** samples of the whole, even if they are parts — complete parts — of the whole. So I would differ from Pratt specifically on this point, which she postulates as a key proposition about the short story, that "the short story is a sample, the novel is the whole hog" (Pratt 1994:102). Perhaps it's a matter of degree rather than of absolutes, but the modern short story seems to me one of the least sample-like uses of language, and that this attenuated 'sample-ness' creates special analytical challenges.

So a story text is not representative of a larger corpus, not context-dependent or context-embedded, and not to be regarded as a sample, in anything like the way that the sequences of classroom discourse analysed thirty years ago by Sinclair and Coulthard (1975) can and even must be so regarded. Part of the authority of the Sinclair and Coulthard analysis of teacher-pupil IRF exchanges rests on our being confident that we could have visited certain classrooms in the West Midlands in the 1970's and witnessed real teachers and pupils tacitly interacting according to the grammar of acts and moves that these linguists identified. That's why the Sinclair-Coulthard findings concerning the patterns of classroom talk, especially of teacher talk, had real-world implications (daunting, or sobering, or whatever).

Nothing parallel applies to Alice Munro's story, entitled 'The Love of a Good Woman': we cannot go to a town called Walley — in where? Northern Ontario? — and look for a couple called Rupert and Enid Quinn. (And still some people are half-inclined to make such pilgrimages, and not entirely absurdly, I think.) This is so foundational a point that I think we sometimes neglect its consequences, one being that, whatever the relation of a Munro story's events and characters may be to real people in the late twentieth century in Canada or elsewhere, that relation is not, or not predominantly, a sampling relation. Because, to repeat, a literary short story is not a sample, it's the whole ball of wax.

4.   Prospection, or Don't Look Back!

In 'Trust the Text', Sinclair emphasizes the importance of focussing on the prospective qualities of discourse. He says this has been usefully applied in studies of spoken discourse (I think he has move-sequences, preference, and adjacency pairs in mind: offer-accept, inform-acknowledge, request-comply, etc.). But he says it has been seriously under-used in analysis of written discourse, where there has been emphasis — too much emphasis — on retrospection (cohesion, repetition, reference, reformulation, etc.). All the lines, links, chains, etc. that we can decorate our texts with during text-analysis, our over-writing of writing, as it were. But Sinclair asks a very simple and therefore very effective question: Can it really be the case that spoken and written are so different that prospection is a key shaper of the former but not of the latter?

Furthermore — and this is where his views are particularly challenging — is retrospection as important to the interpreting of written discourse as received models suggest? How much looking back do we do? We talk of pronouns referring back, but what sort of 'going back' is actually done, by the eyes or the mind? Can we think about these matters and formulate what is done differently, so as to escape from what Sinclair evidently regards as counter-intuitive or even irrational or at least counter to his own introspections, namely the idea that as we advance through a written text, we are frequently going back over what we have just read (the analogy comes to mind of a tide coming in, of the waves in their forward and back motion gradually advancing over the beach — the text — but only with numerous, perhaps rhythmically recurrent, backward scans)? He writes:

> Do we actually need all the linguistic detail of backward reference that we find in text description? Text is often described as a long string of sentences… I would like to suggest, as an alternative, that the most important thing is what is happening in the current sentence. The meaning of any word is got from the state of the discourse and not from where it came from. A word of reference like a pronoun should be interpreted exactly like a proper name or a noun phrase. The reader should find a value for it in the immediate state of the text, and not have to retrieve it from previous text unless the text is problematic at that point.
>
> The state of the discourse is identified with the sentence which is currently being processed. No other sentence is presumed to be available. The previous text is part of the immediately previous experience of the reader or listener, and is no different from any other, non-linguistic, experience. It will normally have lost the features which were used to organize the meaning and to shape the text into a unique communicative instrument.
>
> (Sinclair 2004:13)

This seems to me quite radical, an attempt to break with the static, product-oriented tendencies of most received models. It is also a kind of reaching back to Saussure, and to the second of the two principles of linguistic communication upon which, according to Saussure, everything else in language is built; the first of those principles, much the more dwelt upon not least in critical theory, is the arbitrariness of the sign. The second, which I think Sinclair is here re-invoking, is the

linearity of the sign. A genuinely linear account of language activity (production and reception), as I take this proposal to reflect, addresses the fact that in reality time never stops and there is no going back and that even what we call repetition is no strict 'occurring again for the first time'. We do not normally, in reading, repeatedly go back over what we have just read (and in speech we cannot), so the standard linguistic way of talking about subsequent pronouns 'referring back' to earlier items perhaps tends to foster a misleading account of what is involved. There is some common ground between Sinclair's perspective, focussing on the 'now-ness' of sign production and processing, and Roy Harris's principle of co-temporality (Harris 1981:157–164), the inescapable chronological integration, at the first order of communicative behaviour, of linguistic signification and the surrounding circumstances and interests that prompt the communicative activity in the first place.

The more general idea that reading involves the progressive processing of propositions and referents, which themselves undergo change as the discourse unfolds, is argued for also in Brown and Yule (1983), and in Emmott (1997) and Emmott, Sanford and Morrow (2003). We do not normally 'refer back' in order to interpret pronouns, even if traditional grammars have given the impression that we do; and in fact pronouns in discourse are not a special case. As Sinclair suggests, pronouns in discourse are usually pointing labels just like names, and need — from the point of view of discourse comprehension and processing — no different treatment than all the other kinds of information, lexical and grammatical, that contribute to our developing sense of a text's content, core, plot, theme, and so on. Typically, in longer texts, pronouns are used where series of co-referential linkage to indicated entities and ideas are involved. But as far as processing the currently-read sentence is concerned, interpreting the pronouns will typically involve a lesser effort and attention than that involved in interpreting newly-occurring lexis — but the same kind of effort.

We cannot 'scan back' in speech; we sometimes cannot in face of written text (e.g. where a moving line of text is presented as on various kinds of public display board); and we usually do not when processing written text. 99 times out of 100 we immediately have a confident 'lock' upon who in the text-world is denoted by a *he* or a *she* in the sentence currently being read; on the few occasions that we don't, this will sometimes be due to writer or speaker strategy, but is more often sourced in faulty or divided attention: we have been inattentive, distracted, and therefore read the present sentence or hear the current utterance with what relevance theorists might call a faulty representation of what would ordinarily be manifest to the recipient. Such errors are powerfully displayed in the directions-following map-experiments conducted by Gillian Brown (1995). In certain circumstances you may be able re-trace some discoursal steps, in conversation or reading — but arguably this is always a redundancy or inefficiency. In particular, although linguists sometimes cite the possibility of re-reading for disambiguation and so on as a special virtue of writing, never really possible in speech, one can look at this another way and point out that re-reading is far more palpably inefficient and redundant than any so-called 'loopback' or repair procedures in conversation (where we can advance our comprehension by reformulating — or getting our interlocutor to reformulate — prior uncertainly-understood text). For in the case of written text, as we very well know, there is nothing on the page on our second encounter that wasn't already there the first time around. As Plato long ago noted:

> You'd think [written words] were speaking as if they had some understanding, but if you question anything that has been said because you want to learn more, it continues to signify just that very same thing forever.
>
> (Plato, *Phaedrus* (2001:82))

Hence we really do need to pay more attention, in our model of text-processing, to attention itself: attention to the textualized present 'scene', to our sense (sustained but constantly available for modification) of what is being said now (by what we are reading now).

I think we would do well to ponder at length Sinclair's claims here. They are prefaced by his reminder that, once a text is read, we tend to remember the message but not the actual language. And we can add to this our general recognition that all our past language-using activity is a bit of a blur. That's a remarkable thing, in at least two senses of remarkable. If you try to think back to your most recent conversations prior to reading these words, you are hard pushed, very hard pushed, to remember your own precise words, or those of your interlocutors. And of course it gets worse, the further back one attempts to 'reach'. And very much the same 'rapid dissolve' seems to apply, similarly, to most of our reading (past sentences or phrases that we do not forget deserve a full study on their own). Even speech and writing from the very recent past is a vague blur, with only the gist, or some of the gist, retained.

Therefore there is a powerful psychological reality underpinning Sinclair's idea that everything other than the presently encountered signs is past experience, in memory, and that the window of the presently-encountered may be no wider than the present sentence, the current utterance. What has already been read or heard is gone and lost forever, there is in one sense no going back, and any repeating or re-reading we perform are always a recontextualization: they are conscious acts, contrastable with the relative *un*consciousness with which we listen to a conversation moving forward, or read on through a paragraph. (Again this may be a matter of degree, not kind, high vs. low degrees of reflexivity/consciousness, for example.) So what is going on in the presently-processed sentence, is, indeed, newly crucial.

Much of this is what integrationism refers to in the concept of co-temporality, and there certainly seems to be a congruence between Sinclair's ideas and integrational linguistics in this area.

On the other hand, it may be protested, surely within what Sinclair calls past experience we can distinguish very recent experience, experience still in what psychologists call short term memory for instance? And surely some kind of 'fading hot coal' metaphor might be relevant, to refer to the 'activation' of semantic fields, and a tone, an evaluative stance, themes or macro-propositions, earlier in a text, with every possibility of these key elements being re-activated or reinforced via subsequent mentions? Isn't Sinclair in danger of throwing out the babies, textual coherence and textual structure, with the undesirable bathwater, namely treating the text as a product full of prior stems and references to which the current sentence must repeatedly link back?

Before trying to address these questions let us remind ourselves how absolute Sinclair is:

> From this perspective [identifying the state of the discourse exclusively with whichever sentence is currently being processed], there is no advantage to be gained in tracing the references back in the text. The information thus gleaned will not be relevant to the current state of the discourse because previous states of the text are of no interest to the present state of the text; nor is it important how the present state of the text was arrived at.
>
> (Sinclair 2004: 14)

Again, clear parallels with Saussurean pronouncements regarding the synchronic perspective on *la langue*, and of adopting the language user's perspective, are surely being echoed here.

How, then, does Sinclair proceed, so as to explain the interaction of our already-past experience of prior text with our processing of current text? Unsurprisingly he proposes a role for some form of mental representation of the text so far. But it is not entirely clear to me whether we are being offered a characterization of mental representation, in the paragraph where this concept is alluded to. In the relevant paragraph, the mental representation of a text is said to be describable — very roughly — as "the previous sentence minus its interactive elements..." plus the interpretive inferences it has triggered (p. 14). A first reaction might be to think that perhaps the word *sentence* here should be in the plural, but on reflection this would be inconsistent with the 'one-and-only-one sentence at a time' principle Sinclair is arguing for — itself interestingly echoic of Saussure's linearity principle where it is claimed that speech/language production occurs 'one and only one sign at a time'.

But implications get more daunting before they begin to clarify. Because now Sinclair goes on to say (p. 14) that "The text *is* the sentence that is in front of us when an act of reading is in progress." Each sentence is a new beginning, a new time- and space-bound organization of language and the world. (If sentence and text are definitionally synonymous, he adds parenthetically, this 'resolves' the paradoxes or problems we have defining the sentence — the tension between it being a complete thought and also obviously only a part of a larger complete whole. Again I'm not sure that all is so clearly resolved. In particular if each new sentence is a new text, what do we call the collectivity of such sentences: a text of texts?).

5.   Prior text as context, present text as communicative

What I like about this paper is the sense of a very creative mind inching forward on a topic where it seems to be very easy, and very common, to become satisfied with obfuscatory metaphor or received opinion or untestable abstraction. So what Sinclair says next is fascinating since it seems to resist those three traps. He suggests that as readers we treat the current sentence as containing just one connection with preceding states of the text, "a single act of reference" that "encapsulates the whole of the previous text and simultaneously removes its interactive potential", all past sentences are "represented simply as part of the shared knowledge" one invariably brings to bear on current interpretation (p. 14). Some kind of indexical link is made, and repeatedly updated with each passing sentence; the link is to one's mental model of the text so far, the story so far, this being conceived as the background, the framework, the context, in relation to which the current and only text, in the foreground, is interpreted. I like the sound of all this. And it rings true, to me, to imply as Sinclair does that you can't be attending, interactively, to pages 16 and 17 if you are actually reading lines on page 18. It's hard enough, in integrated activities involving speech, to respond to a seminar colleague's request to focus the projector and at the same time make an apology to latecomers for not bringing enough handouts. Some of us, some of the time, can manage that kind of 'multi-tasking'; but writing imposes such conditions that reading two sentences at once (let alone three or more) is impossible. It is linearity or co-temporality all the way down.

This large, radical hypothesis, Sinclair suggests at the top of p. 15, might enable us to concentrate in description on the communicative function of each sentence and not to worry about its textual antecedents. And what **that** means, what the communicative function of a sentence means, we must now find out.

At this point he returns to the quirky sentence, *The implications are daunting*, and re-examines it in its co-text:

> The Japanese use western languages not merely to market their goods but to improve their products by studying those of their rivals. [1] The implications are daunting. [2] Not merely must the business have personnel with skills in different languages but the particular languages and the degree of skill may vary from person to person according to his or her job within the business. [3] They may also vary from decade to decade as new markets open up in different countries. [4]
>   (Sinclair 2004:15)

In sentence (2) here, it is suggested that the very use of the phrase *the implications* renders the whole of the preceding sentence whatever it is that has implications. And sentence (2) also prospects, telling us in advance that what follows *are* the implications. Sentence (3) does not contain an act of reference (to 1, 2, etc.), the reason being that it is 'fully prospected by its predecessor' — just as in speech an answer may be fully prospected by the question and therefore not contain an act of reference to the question.

On the strength of such evidence, Sinclair proposes that each sentence in a text has potential for a single act of reference, unless that sentence is fully prospected by its predecessor. Each sentence can also prospect, and whatever is prospected "remains pertinent" (but not communicationally active) until fulfilled or deflected.

Sentence 1: may prospect
Sentence 2: may prospect, but may also make encapsulated reference to everything previous

So in the following five-move invented service exchange, the prospections involved at each move may be as glossed here in italics:

> A   **Can I have a ham and cheese ciabatta please.** *Prospects some kind of reply/ response*
> B   **To eat in or take away?** *Fully prospected by prior, also prospects*
> A   **Take away.** *Fully prospected by prior*
> B   **[While handing over the ciabatta] Two pounds fifty please.** *No act of reference, fully prospected by turn 1; also prospects act of payment*
> A   **[Gives exact money]** *Prospected by previous, no act of reference*

Now follow some remarks about descriptions of the higher organization of language, which he notes has remained largely "at the stage of patterns and labels. Little has been done to describe restrictions or to explain the reasons for the patterns, that is, to make a proper structural description" (p. 16). He mentions stylistics in particular, interestingly. And he adds "It is not enough that a particular description of language can actually provide a set of boxes into which text can be apportioned. We must look for models which help the text to reveal itself to us". Turning again to the new technologies, and computer-aided text analysis, he warns that we have been so used to interpreting scant evidence that we may be ill-equipped to cope with the new situation, where evidence may be in too plentiful supply: "With the new evidence the main difficulty is controlling and organizing it rather than getting it" (p. 17).

There follow a couple of pages in which some of the general findings of the Cobuild researches c. 1990 are alluded to, and then in the final pages of the article Sinclair returns to some quite broad and again thought-provoking ideas. Many stem from his wanting to take collocation really seriously. He notes that one way of describing collocation is to say that "the choice of one word conditions the choice of the next, and of the next again" (p. 19). This leads to what appears to be advocacy of a non-discrete or non-morphemic analysis of textual meanings:

> Successive meanings can be discerned in the text, and you can associate a meaning or component of meaning or a shade of meaning with this or that word or phrase that is present in the text. But it is often impossible in the present state of our knowledge to say precisely where the realization of that meaning starts and stops, or exactly which pattern of morphemes is responsible for it (p. 19).

Is this a current difficulty or a permanent characteristic? The latter, Sinclair suspects: "I think there probably is in language an interesting indeterminacy". Text-composition is not (or not chiefly) a matter of word-by-word independent selection, but selection of multi-word spans or phases, informed by syntagmatic prospection. And a grammar or model that does not acknowledge this common and ordinary degree of pre-assembly of multi-word chunks will seriously overstate the amount of 'meaningful choice' that a language-user normally has recourse to. Of subliminal idioms such as *an accident of* (*birth, nature, society...*) he says "we understand them as centring on a slightly specialized meaning of a word in a common grammatical environment and in a regular collocation" (p. 22).

Finally, again looking at *implications* and *daunting*, Sinclair curiously says he doesn't know what other things can be *daunting* besides *implications*. I would suggest that *tasks, facts, undertakings, prospects, workloads* and *schedules* can all be daunting, in the singular as well as the plural. And indeed the Bank of English confirms that all these, along with various processes expressed as full clauses, collocate with *daunting*. But the corpus springs a surprise on me when it reveals that a shirt can be daunting: *You, too, could be protected when you wear this daunting shirt* (from US ephemera, a 'What on Earth' catalogue). And implications where not daunting, can alternatively be *ludicrous, hilarious, sobering, serious, tragic*, or *offensive* (or, the corpus reveals, *political, ethical*, and mostly followed by *of* or *for*).

Still I think Sinclair is right to say that a subliminal idiom is at work in *daunting implications*, something not far off a cliché, the kind of thing that allows a degree of what I have elsewhere called pre-reading. There is a degree of co-selection of *implications* and *daunting* and *daunting* is a "member of an odd lemma" (p. 22) in that there are no finite forms such as *you daunt*. But these things are so often a matter of degree (consider *disturbing*, for example, which also co-selects with *implications*).

But what, now, should we make of the fact that when the 450 million word Bank of English is searched for instances of *implications* followed immediately, or within up to four words, by *daunting*, that no instances are reported? And that only one instance is found of *daunting* followed (within 4 words to right) by *implications*? That solitary instance is:

> high long term unemployment — with daunting implications for German's wobbling public finances (*Economist* 93 03 27)

In short, although there are numerous instances of *implications* in the Bank of English, and quite a few also of *daunting*, there seems to be only one instance recorded of their co-occurrence; wherever our sense of their phraseological attraction comes from, our sense that *daunting* primes us for *implications*, we would not have it were we to have only encountered the Bank's 450 million words. This might prompt circumspection lest we overstate the strength of particular phraseological collocations, and even of the phraseological tendency. (Certainly particular instances, such as the alleged negative prosody of *weather* and *set in* such that talking about the *good weather setting in* is said to 'sound wrong' or surely ironical, need substantial qualification in my view.) However it may also prompt us to speculate whether '*implications…daunting*' might not be more common in speech than in writing, and that indeed quite a few of our received associations of words in multi-word phrases are mainly reinforced by speech, where composing 'at your own pace' and autonomous item by item is less often an option.

6. Conclusions

'Trust the Text' is a paper of rare originality, a paper that takes risks and prompts the reader to think in a new way about an issue that is as old as the hills, the reading of texts. It is work in progress, making a number of speculations and suggestions, which are obviously in need of further discussion, further testing, further conversion into some form that can be tested and falsified. It is full of daunting implications. For these very reasons, it is relatively light on hard facts, heavy on speculations — just the kind of balance, ironically, that is criticized in its opening paragraphs. And it certainly provides very little evidence for its ideas about written sentences as carrying at most one reference while prospecting future sentences to a greater or lesser degree. So there are quite a few paradoxes here. I'm still puzzling, in my own mind, about just how much is really at stake in the opposition between the view outlined in the paper, and old-style text-analysis with its links and referring back. Maybe the difference boils down to a contrast between a model which talks about a text-medial sentence referring back and referring forward in a variety of lexical and grammatical ways (names, pronouns, settings, likely subsequent actions, etc.) and a model which talks about a reader, upon encountering that sentence, interpreting the sentence in light of the mental representation they have in mind and to which they can add by means of recall of past experience and predictions of textual/semantic continuation.

I hope to have suggested that there are many challenging ideas in the 'Trust the Text' paper, and that it will rightly go into anthologies of seminal but sometimes cryptic position statements in the post-Firthian tradition, as the years go by. Still I wonder if I entirely grasp why Sinclair emphasized *trust*, in the paper's title. Legal trusts are a kind of future performative: I hereby give (when, after my death, my grandchildren reach the age of majority) such and such property. Does Sinclair have some analogy to this in mind, when he talks about reading and analysing text? I suppose I could look up *trust* in a dictionary, but would it help? I did look for instances of *trust+the+text* in the 450-million word Bank of English, and found just two occurrences, which rapidly reduced to one, as the second instance straddled a sentence boundary (*understanding and trust. The text uses the term 'hansei'…*). The one true instance comes, thought-provokingly enough, in a humorous journalistic piece by writer Michael Frayn, writing in the *Guardian* about the curious artificiality you sense when you record yourself on your telephone answering machine, for the benefit of future callers — "There's nobody here at present", you begin, absurdly enough:

> You know you are talking to yourself, and you have begun to feel rather foolish. Like an actor on a bad night, you find that your whole performance is beginning to break up around you. You are not speaking politely or impatiently, confidently or cautiously. You are speaking slowly and carefully. That unresponding audience out there …you have a sudden uneasy feeling that it may not even understand English. **You don't trust the text any more.** And so you start to try and improve upon it. "You have reached 0467 22 983 3451," you say, very distinctly. This is odd — you've never announced your number to me before. You don't need to. I know it. I've just dialled it.
> (Michael Frayn, 'First person-tell us everything', *The Guardian*, NB3 95 01 04. [Bold added])

Or, less legal-mindedly, we talk of trust when we set aside self-protecting conditions, go forward relying on the person (or structure, or text, perhaps) that we are leaning on: we commit ourselves. That may well be what Sinclair has in mind; in which case I would see it as chiming well with Gricean cooperative assumptions, and even 'orientedness to other' (Toolan 1996). Perhaps, Sinclair wishes to complain, we are too distrustful of the power of texts, of their ability to lead us towards their ends, without disruptions, re-readings, hidden meanings, and so on. Of course some texts need to be read this distrustfully or suspiciously, have been designed to be so (insurance policies come to mind for some reason), but that cannot be the norm, anymore than lying can be the conversational norm. Texts are better designed, are more straightforward, than that. We look for the wrong kind of complexity, and an objectified, product-assuming complexity, if we distrust the text; whereas the collocational and prospective evidence (of which there is no shortage) suggests that texts are smoothly progressing discourses.

References

Brown, G. (1995). *Speakers, Listeners and Communication: Explorations in Discourse Analysis.* Cambridge: Cambridge University Press.

Brown, G. & Yule, G. (1983). *Discourse Analysis.* Cambridge: Cambridge University Press.

Emmott, C. (1997). *Narrative Comprehension: a Discourse Perspective.* Oxford: Oxford University Press.

Emmott, C., Sanford, A. & Morrow, L. (2003). Towards a theory of reading in the age of cognitive science. *Belgian Journal of English Language and Literatures,* n.s. 1, 17–30.

Fairclough, N. (1992). *Discourse and Social Change.* Cambridge: Polity Press.

Haiman, J. (1998). *Talk is Cheap: Sarcasm, Alienation and the Evolution of Language.* Oxford: Oxford University Press.

Harris, R. (1981). *The Language Myth.* London: Duckworth.

Plato (2001). *Phaedrus.* Translated with introduction and notes by A. Nehamas & P. Woodruff. Indianapolis: Hackett, c1995.

Pratt, M. L. (1994). The short story: the long and the short of it. In C. May (Ed.), *The New Short Story Theories* (pp. 91–113). Athens, OH: Ohio University Press.

Sinclair, J. M. (2004). *Trust the Text: Language, Corpus and Discourse.* London: Routledge. (Chapter 1, 'Trust the text', was first published in 1992 in L. Ravelli & M. Davies (Eds.), *Systemic Advances in Systemic Linguistics: Recent Theory and Practice,* London: Pinter; and republished in 1994 in M. Coulthard (Ed.), *Advances in Written Text Analysis,* London: Routledge.)

Sinclair, J. M. & Coulthard, R. M. (1975). *Towards an Analysis of Discourse: the English Used by Teachers and Pupils.* London: Oxford University Press.

Toolan, M. (1996). *Total Speech: An Integrational Linguistic Approach to Language.* Durham and London: Duke University Press.

Widdowson, H. (1995). Discourse analysis: a critical view. *Language and Literature,* 4 (3), 157–172.

Subject Index

In the series *Benjamins Current Topics (BCT)* the following titles have been published thus far or are scheduled for publication: